The End is Not Near

It's Here

Lawson Media Services

ONLINE SOLUTIONS FOR BUSINESS SUCCESS

Branding | Logo | Publishing | eCommerce | Marketing | Responsive Web Design

The End is Not Near

It's Here

*Israel, Jerusalem, Alternative Lifestyles,
Earthquakes, Natural Disasters,
and How it All Relates to You*

by

Apostle Lee E. Gaddie

The End Is Not Near It's Here

© Copyright 2019 – Apostle Lee E. Gaddie

ALL RIGHTS RESERVED

Published by:

Lawson Media Services

12680 W Lake Houston Pkwy., Ste. 510-4006

Houston, Texas 77044

LawsonMediaServices.com

866-82-LAWSON (52976)

ISBN-13: 978-0692155028

ISBN-10: 0692155023

Dedication

To my beautiful wife, Prophetess Pearly Gaddie.

No one could know the trials she has faced with me through the years. Nevertheless, she has remained faithful. I thank God for her. If she had not been willing to stand by me until I came to the place of full surrender to the will of God for my life, I am not sure what might have happened to me. This day would not have been possible without her determination and dedication. Through everything, she stuck close by my side.

Contents

Foreword

I am excited to introduce you to a masterpiece, inspired by God and written by Bishop Lee Gaddie.

The book that you hold in your hands is a labor of love and inspiration from the Holy Spirit. Allow God to show you, your role in these End Times, which is being revealed in this body of work.

Pastor Gaddie is sharing a deep revelation on the biblical significance of current world events as the signs pointing our attention to Jesus' return to earth. As you read, you will discover that disastrous events you hear in the news are not just happenstances but clues to the fulfillment of both Bible's prophecies and Jesus Christ's prophecies about the fate of the Church, satan, humanity, and the earth.

~

Pastor Gaddie's insight on these present perilous times is like the voice of Issachar, a tribe of Israel whom the Bible says understood the seasons and times, and as a result, all other tribes gave heed to their instructions. Every reader of this book would do well to take heed to the revelation herein.

You will be blessed, informed, and excited about your role in God's calendar of events to come.

This man of God will lay out for you the events of today and those to come and how they work in conjunction with Scripture.

Be blessed as you turn each page in amazement, that you get to live in this day of the Lord.

~ Prophetess Sandra Seal

Preface

The End Times as a topic has always been a controversial and difficult terrain for most people. It is a type of writing that requires extensive or scholarly knowledge of the Bible. According to the Lord's leading, I have been able to jot down something to remind the world about the times we are in; these are things to come and how to escape the coming desolation and pain.

This book will not only inform Christians, but it will also educate those who are not Christians about the "sign of the times" that have been talked about for years.

This is not a sermon. We already have enough sermon notes and recordings we can transcribe regarding this subject. This book is written to correlate what the bible said would happen and how God's truth is presenting itself in our lives and our children's lives.

News headlines daily inundate us with talks of wars, natural disasters, political calamity, and social impoverishment; and people all around the world are suffering regardless of their religion and socioeconomic status. These reports and news headlines should urge us to heed the Scriptures empathically.

The event of Israel becoming a nation in 1948 signifies the beginning of the end as most biblical scholars would agree. The nations continue to experience advancements towards a one-world government. Also, false teachings, perils, and calamities, countries rising against each other, and plagues are just a few of what is talked about in the Scriptures as signs to watch out for.

Although these things must happen according to Scripture, they let us know to prepare ourselves and our families as Christians and to inform others about what is happening and how the sacrifice of Jesus saves us all.

The End Time is still to come, and I want to speak to the people that are here on this earth now to let them know that they do not have to fear. Scripture has forewarned us. There is a way of escape! Only believe and accept Jesus.

Introduction

With the level of troubles that the human race is contending with, from wars, natural disasters, political turmoil, to economic woes, we wonder if humanity will ever survive. The Scripture reveals great truth about the long-prophesied events of the end times that will signal the Second Coming of Jesus Christ!

It is almost upon us—the Great Tribulation with the antichrist. As troubling as this information is, it breaks my heart to see people refusing to accept that we are on the eve of destruction.

The Weeks of Years is dealing with the last seven years. Christ comes during the middle, three and a half years after it begins, and gets his people. He raptures the church out. The antichrist goes into the temple and says that he is the christ, the messiah for the people. The antichrist is the abomination that causes desolation to come. In short, this will cause all hell to break loose upon the earth and the inhabitants who are left. The saints will be in heaven rejoicing while the earth is judged.

The time of great trouble and devastation that is soon to be inflicted on us is so great that the Bible says that nothing like this has ever happened on the earth in all of man's more than 6,000 years on it. The Scripture confirms that this horrifying physical tribulation will take place [for three and a half years].

On the very last day of the time mentioned, the greatest of all destruction, like an avalanche, will sweep man away. It will be so huge that the combination of World War 1 and World War 2 will be child's play in comparison to this catastrophe. The Lord God Himself will on that day bring death, destruction, and judgment upon the earth and its remaining inhabitants. After that period, Jesus Christ will return to this earth accompanied by His members of God's Family to reign over all the earth. The world then will be under a new order with a single world government—the Millennial Reign of Christ.

It is prophesied in the Bible that most people will not believe what is about to happen, not even if the world is plunged into the most significant destruction and violence it has ever experienced. The possibility that these events will come to pass may be too much for our human mind to make sense of and accept right now; maybe that is the reason some do not want to believe it.

After church service one day, I sat in my office recalling and thanking God for His presence in the service. As I prepared to leave one of the members who recently graduated high school approached me at the door. He explained that he did not prepare for a test. This test was important, and he needed to make a nearly perfect score to keep his GPA up high enough to attend the college of his choice. He said he ignored his parents advise to prepare for the test; instead, he chose to enjoy the last weeks of high school attending senior activities and parties. Even with that, he had time to study but did not. Before long, the day of the test was upon him and he knew he was not prepared. When the class began, and the teacher passed out the test, the students were all instructed that the exam would be an open book test due to it being a comprehensive exam and that they would have an extended class period to complete the test. Relieved, he ended that his lack of preparation reminded him of God's grace.

One thing I would like you to understand is this: God has provided us an open book to what is to come. It would be wise of you to know of the signs to look for and take precaution so that when it does happen, as prophesied, your salvation will be your saving grace.

Not only has the enormity of these events been foretold, but also there are prophecies on the specific nations and areas of the earth where these cataclysms and plagues will take place. God is so exact and precise about what is going to happen that He even gave estimations of the human population that will escape in certain countries.

You cannot, according to your likes and dislikes, reject or ignore what is written in this book. Unfortunately, a more substantial portion of the world will reject and ignore it, the same way they did in the times of Noah. There are even people who still think the story of Noah is a fiction. It is true whether you choose to believe it or not. Noah and his family were mocked beyond words in those days. The mockery ended abruptly when the waters began to rise. The floods continued in their upward rise resulting in every mocker and their families' death. Please do not wait until it becomes too late for you to act as it happened to those people in the times of Noah.

Global destruction of epic proportions is coming, but unlike in the days of Noah, this time around, millions will get the chance to live in the New World. If you are bold enough to mock what is written here, then you too will miss the opportunity to partake of the New World when it finally happens.

This is not a popular message, and never will be because satan *"hath blinded their eyes and hardened their heart; that they should not see with their eyes, nor understand with their heart, and be converted..."* (John 12:40). Nonetheless, it is true, and it will come to pass as foretold. Our desires or popular demands cannot sway God. After more than 6,000 years, the time is, has always been, and will continue to be here for man to listen to God. For many years, my wife has been known by all that she meets to say these words of admonishment to them: *"Get Ready, Stay Ready, and Be Ready."* This is the common thread I want every reader to consider. I will tell you more about this revelation she received from God later in the book.

I am sure you have heard of the numerous times that the church has warned that the time is coming. I understand that the time aspect can get confusing and cause some to not believe in the truth and power of the word of God. I encourage you to take head of the Scriptures. Do not lean to your understanding. Seek God continually, and He will guide your path.

The warning being spoken of here will be told with greater power during the final three and a half years. Two witnesses will appear on the scene, backed by God's power with miracles and signs, and they will boldly speak about the same things written in the pages of this book.

The Manifestation of God's Will

After the flood in Genesis, the Lord told His children to be scattered abroad and replenish the earth. They defied God and conspired with each other to build a city to live in and a tower to reach up to heaven so they could be remembered. They did not have God's will as the basis for their decision. Likewise, we do not have God's will as the basis for our choices. We have already begun implementing the foundation for a one-world government, one-world system, that does not have God in the center of it. There is nothing new under the sun. When they tried to reach Heaven, God came down and said the people had become one. Then God decided to confound their tongs so that they could not understand one another. God's will so impressed upon the people for generations that when Pentecost occurred, and the Holy Ghost fell, the people who heard the Galatians speaking in other languages of the mighty things of God assumed the people in the house were drunkards. God took languages and scattered the people. Then he took words in the 2nd chapter of Acts and brought the people back together. The map below from BishopMike.com is a map representation of the countries of people mentioned at Pentecost.

Since humanity's attempt to defy God's command, we have been separated by desserts, oceans, customs, ideologies, opinions, language, traditions, walls, and cultural barriers. We will always witness the manifestation of God's will upon this earth, regardless of the peoples' intentions. Bringing the people back together is what we are looking at now and trusting

God to do. We have our part to play in this last act. I
will say again: *The End is Not Near...It's Here.*

Countries of People Mentioned at Pentecost

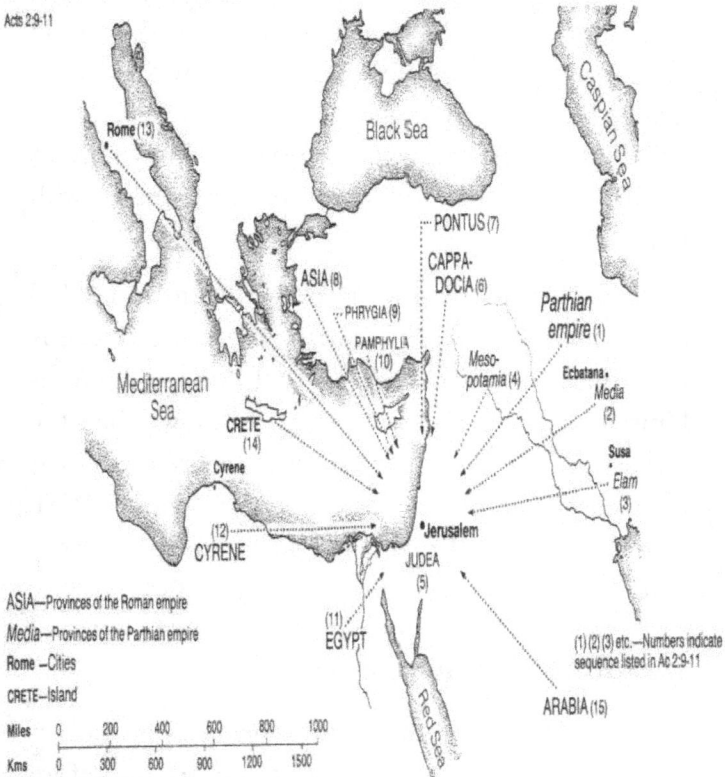

*Figure 1 Map: Map of the countries of people
mentioned at Pentecost according to the Book of
Acts Chapter 2 and verses 9-11.*

Source: Courtesy of BishopMike.com

My wife had a revelation from God several years ago about us being ready for God. She has shared this with many, and now I share it with you. This book is not to bring fear, but it is to admonish us all to get ready, be ready, and stay ready, for no man knows the hour or the time that God will come. God has given us the signs of the times to know that we are getting closer. Even so, we are all born, and surely, we will die, this is a fact. I encourage you to live your best life in God. Accept and establish a relationship with him.

Failure to prepare is preparing to fail. God always gives warnings to let us know that the time is near. We do not know the day nor the hour, even Jesus himself said that He nor the angels know when the Father speaks. People have set days according to their calculations of biblical end-time predictions. Well, those days have all come and gone, and we are still here. It is time for us to prepare to meet God.

Headline: Hungry in America

The media headlines are causing us to look at the events that are taking place on earth right before our very eyes—in real-time. Look at the disasters, the earthquakes, the floods. When you turn on the news, you see and hear of all the events that are happening. You do not have to be a rocket scientist to understand that these events are not typical. Russia, China, Syria, the United States, and all the nations are working within God's timetable. These things are happening just the way God said they would happen. Bible prophecies are revealing themselves truly as these events happen more and more frequently. The end is right here; it is close.

When a woman goes through her trimesters of pregnancy, she goes through various phases. However, when she gets down to the end, she experiences birth pains. She must go through the pain to see the promise. The closer the labor pains, the sooner the child will be born. Just like a woman who is birthing a child during the last phase, the baby must crown. You can see the head, but it has not come forth yet. Likewise, the nations and this world are in birth pains. The crowning of destruction and disaster has created traveling screams that reverberate throughout the earth.

When I was a young boy at the age of twelve years old, I had a vision of the coming of the Lord. The sight shook me to the core. I was in my hometown of Sweet Home, Arkansas near Little Rock. It was a typical day for me as I walked down the street. Suddenly, the sky opened as if it were the opening of the curtains for a leading, grand act. I saw Jesus at the center of millions and millions of angels. His radiance shined like a solitary diamond. I was never the same afterward. I began to tell people about what I saw.

Many whom I confided in told me I would be a preacher. I did not want to be a preacher and stopped telling others about it. Little did I know that God used the vision he gave as a germinating seed of faith that has grown me to the man I am today, and which will continue to grow me in Him. From that day forth, God has genuinely dealt and worked with me. When I was in my early twenties, God spoke to me, and He said that He likened me unto Moses & Elijah. At that time in my life, I did not understand what God meant.

The Bible says Moses sought to deliver the children of Israel when he was forty years of age. Moses killed an Egyptian man and had to run for his life. He was there on the backside of the desert for another 40 years. Moses was 80 years of age when God's timing perfected itself for him to carry out God's will. Understand that no one is above anyone else in Gods eyes. We all have a specific purpose on this earth that God has ordained for each of us to help carry out and move forth His will and plan.

I went through some things in my life, and now I am in my seventies. The Lord told me that at the later part of my life He was going to release me to do the work that he predestined me to do. God has used me to do miraculous manifested evidence of his healing and deliverance power. God has delivered people from stage four cancer, instantaneous weight loss, and crippled have not walked but ran after God's power fell on them. The healings that I have witnessed is just the tip of the iceberg. Jesus said in John 14:12 that we will do "greater works" than He. We have barely touched all that God can do. We all have the right to not only receive His salvation but to also live our lives witnessing to the benefits that God provides.

My wife and I were in Memphis, Tennessee, over 40 years ago attending a church service. We noticed a peculiar lady walking back and forth. She shouted, "*hungry in America,*" repeatedly. Like Noah, many people hear God's peculiar people cry out the truth in hopes of our souls being saved, but many will not listen. Her words struck a chord within our spirits and we have always kept her words in our thoughts and prayers.

Since then, we have witnessed many times of unexpected food shortages created by disasters and disease. Ten years ago, one of the church members had a vision of people running to the stores with barrels of money and coming out with a few bags of food. She informed the church that she believed her vision meant for us to prepare and stock our cupboards and to also not rely on our government to provide food but to begin to grow our own food. I believe this to be a vison from God and one we all must take heed to. There may come a time when there is not enough to go around and hunger in America will be the norm.

I read David Wilkerson's book in 1974 called The Vision. He said they would call him an alarmist, but his purpose was to explain to us what God has shown him. He spoke of the headlines using descriptive words such as "*unprecedented*," and this is what many have been saying. The disasters are happening but have never occurred in this intensity before. The United States has the wherewithal to tackle any natural disaster with our military strength and money to follow, however; with people young and old dying by the droves in disasters and wars, our strength in power will soon be debilitated by the loss of our strength in numbers.

When we look at just the recent past years, 2017, 2018, and now 2019. We continually hear and see of all the disasters and calamities and how rapid things have happened one behind the other on national scales that I talk about in this book. Only God knows what will be in 2020. Based on the trend, surely more is to come. There is no telling what this year will do. I encourage you to build a relationship with Christ Jesus. His well of help and His protection will never run dry.

End-Time Assignment

My assignment is End Time. Many do not realize this, but everyone has an assignment. They may not know what it is but Paul, when he was on the Damascus road, heard the Lord speak to him. The

Lord stopped him and called his name twice, Saul, Saul, why persecute thou me. He said, "*who art thou Lord.*" God replied, "*I am Jesus whom you persecute.*" he asked, "*what would you have me to do?*" he was asking God what his assignment was. Saul was a terrorist. The church was terrified of him. Then God changed his name from Saul to Paul. Who would have believed that this same man would be credited for writing one-third of the books in the Bible? Paul's life change goes to show that it is not how you start; it is how you end. We should strive to realize what is our calling. What is the purpose that God would have for us to do?

In addition to the vision that God gave me as a 12-year-old boy, another major event in my life that helped to propel me to accept the call on my life happened before I was an adult. My brother fell from a Hickory tree, and he had brain damage. He suffered horrifically. Back in the 1950s, medical care was not as advanced as it is today. Medicine was not as readily available as it is today. We were told that the only thing the doctors could do was to keep him comfortable due to brain injury. My brother had multiple seizures every day. It was tough to continue even normal daily activities and not feel helpless for what my brother had to endure. I would hear my brother crying throughout the night due to the immense pain he was in. One Sunday morning, as we prepared for church, my father pulled me aside and said, "*when you get back from church, your brother will be gone.* " Well, I did not fully understand what he was speaking of because I could not imagine where my brother would be going.

Although I did not understand what my Father was saying, his words made me recall the words I had spoken to God a few nights beforehand. My first prayer that I ever prayed was because of my brother. I said, *"Now Lord, they say that you are God and that you can help people. I want you to help my brother, and if you do not help my brother, I will not serve you. However, if you help my brother, I will serve you."* I did not know at that time what I had prayed. I did not realize that I was making a vow to God. I pondered on those words that I spoke and the words that my Father spoke during the entire church service. Little did I know; my dad saw death on my brother. When we got back home after church that Sunday afternoon, my brother was deceased.

After we laid my brother to rest, I felt a weight lifted. I no longer felt helpless. I understood that he was in a better place and that he was no longer in pain. He had no more suffering. He may not have lived many years on this earth, but his assignment helped to propel me into what God had called me to do. I am sure he had many more people lives that he touched, encouraged, and inspired; I merely recall what his life did for me and my purpose. We have assignments, and they will affect various people in different ways. Think about the last wedding ceremony, birthday celebration, awards presentation, or funeral you attended. Now recall the central theme that everyone seemed to speak about the person of celebration. He or she usually touch many lives in different capacities, but everyone regularly appears to have an underlying similarity that they were known for—we can be safe to call this that person assignment. Our assignment is something that we intrinsically have. You cannot see it, yet you know the fruit of it manifested here on this earth. Our assignment is given by God to help us carry out the will of God and fulfill God's purpose in His timing. God uses our personality, gifts, characteristics, attributes, nationality, talents, and more to propel us into the assignment He has for us. Though God uses the things about us, we must understand that our assignment is not about us. When we walk in the true calling of our assignment, we walk in selflessness. We yield our will over to God and enjoy in the fruit that comes from walking in purpose and calling—our God-given assignment.

God held His end of my vow. He helped my brother. I knew that my brother was in a better place, but I was still dealing with the sadness of losing a loved one and a loved one that was so young. I faded in and out of acceptance and denial over the circumstances of my brother's death. I began to run from God. I did not surrender, nor did I desire to serve God at that time. Many things transpired in my life, and it was not until I was about twenty-one that I had to come full circle on my vow to God. After high school, I joined the Army and had various things that happen to me overseas. On several different occasions, I was almost killed. Then cancer reared its head on me, and I had gone down in weight and was deathly ill. God spared me through it all, and I knew it was only God. I had met my pastor on my job, and he ministered to me about coming to the Lord. When I turned my life over to the Lord, He healed me. God sparing me was nothing short of several miraculous stories. I survived many things, and I know I should not have survived. God's long-suffering with me has brought me to this place.

The Manifestation of the Sons of God

The body of Christ will experience a momentous movement in the power of God. It is like the Great Awakening as new believers come to know Christ through His miraculous healing power with signs and wonders. All are pointing towards His coming, and there will be a great revival before He comes back.

The world is waiting on the manifestation of the sons of God. We are the silent giant. We are quiet when the world is protesting, marching, and rationalizing their worldly views. God is setting this in place to make moves that will ignite the church worldwide as a whole. The persecution of Christians will ramp up as the world strengthens itself and leans to their understanding. There will also be a great falling away and the rebellion of God's truth by the church. We, as God's people need to rise and get in the place that God wants us to be.

There is an escape for you if you will only trust in the Lord Jesus to save your soul from sin. Only He can save you from the impending great trial and tribulation.

You can escape the great trial and great tribulation that is coming on this evil generation by trusting in the Lord Jesus to save you from your sins.

I have given each reader a lot to think about in just this introduction alone. You may wonder why. Why is the introduction so long? I have come to an understand that a text must be of great interest or show the reader how they fit into the narrative. Although lengthy, I want the introduction to show realistic real-life scenarios on how we all fit into the narrative of the End Times. It is my prayer that I have garnered your attention and piqued your interest so that you feel compelled to continue reading and learning so that you and your loved ones are prepared to rejoice on the winning side of God!

CHAPTER ONE

End Time Sign Posts

I n the book of Matthew 24:3, it is written, *"And as he sat upon the Mount of Olives, the disciples came unto him privately, saying, Tell us, when shall these things be? And what shall be the sign of thy coming, and of the end of the age?"*

Before Jesus was born, there were many prophecies in the Jewish Scriptures about the coming of a Messiah. Some of these prophecies described a Messiah that would be coming to rid the world of unbelievers and idolaters. Others described Him as someone who would suffer at the hands of men and die to wipe away our sins.

Before His birth, the Jewish people examined the Messianic prophecies to know what God would do. Many of these Jewish scholars did not fully understand these prophecies. They did not realize that the predictions were talking about the Messiah coming at two separate times. According to Isaiah 52:13-15 and 53:1-12, the first coming of the Messiah would be to redeem man to the Father by dying on the cross so that He would come in the role of a servant.

From Jeremiah 23:5-6 and Daniel 7:13-14, we understand that His second coming will be in a kingly manner, as the deliverer of God's people, and the ultimate conqueror of all evil. Sadly, according to Acts 1:6, many Jewish people only looked for and waited for the kingly Messiah who would save them from the tyranny of the Roman Empire. And because the prophecies of a coming servant Messiah did not fit their view of a kingly Messiah, they either ignored the prophecies or misapplied them – the same as what many of us are doing today.

As a result of this, when Jesus finally came, the Jewish people thought He was the kingly Messiah who would set up the Kingdom of God in Jerusalem. This belief is evident in their spreading of clothes and palm branches, a few days before Passover, to mark His triumphant entry into Jerusalem, and the people were shouting and crying, *"Hosanna: Blessed is the King of Israel that cometh in the name of the Lord"* (John 12:13). As revealed in John 19:14-15, when this same Jesus could not fulfill their understanding of the prophecies, the Jewish people turned against Him and demanded His death. *"And it was the preparation of the Passover, and about the sixth hour: and he saith unto the Jews, Behold your King! However, they cried out, away with him, away with him, crucify him. Pilate saith unto them, Shall I crucify your King? The chief priests answered we have no king but Caesar."* They thought he was a kingly Messiah but were disappointed that He was a servant, Messiah. So, they rejected Him.

When it comes to scriptural prophecies, the Jewish people made these two common mistakes: first, believing that the fundamental purpose of prophecy was the description of what would take place in the future; secondly, creating and adding too many assumptions from their limited understanding of these prophecies. Many Jewish people were not aware of the prophecies being fulfilled because the fulfillment of it did not align with their expectations. Therefore, we must be cautious when studying End Time prophecies, so as not to fall into the same ditch.

The Bible says in Luke chapter 21 and verse 36 to *"watch...and pray always that you may be accounted worthy to escape ALL these things that shall come to pass [upon the earth], and standing before the Son of Man."* The Lord has reassured us that we, His children, are not going through tribulations.

Do you understand the geological areas such as the West Bank is Judea? The Iranians are the Persians. Names have changed, but the Bible says there is no new thing done under the sun—this is indeed true. We have a more sophisticated or elaborate way of doing things. What I say about things of this world not being new sets the tone for the fact that although we see things as happening in this world as new or more intense does not mean that is it new to God. As Christians, we have a belief that everything that happens, happens for a reason. God uses the happenings of this world for His good. With the signs of the times that we see daily, God is indeed using these things for His good.

All through the Scriptures, many End Time prophecies have been laid out for God's people. There are two things we must note about these prophecies. Number one, we should rest assured that God is aware of all, that He is not taken by surprise, and that He is in control of the situation (John 13:19, 14:29, and 16:4).

Number two, they let us know where we are in the plan of God. In this way, we can refer to prophecies as city signs. They are designed to catch our attention and give us proper notice of the warnings ahead. Bible prophecies are God's living word placed before us in the right place at the right time to provide us incite to what is to come.

One great example is the Abomination of Desolation. This event will tell us when we are about to enter the Great Tribulation as described in Matthew 24:15 and 21, "*When ye, therefore, shall see the abomination of desolation, spoken of by Daniel the prophet, stand in the holy place, (whoso readeth, let him understand). For then shall be great tribulation, such as was not since the beginning of the world to this time, no, nor ever shall be.*" We may not know, ahead of time, when the Great Tribulation will begin, but when we experience the Abomination of Desolation, we will know that the Great Tribulation has begun.

The Gospel, according to Matthew 24:15, tells us the importance of understanding the prophecy concerning the Abomination of Desolation. Apart from the Abomination of Desolation showing us when we have gotten to a specific time in history, it also does the work of assuring us that the enemy's work does not take God by surprise.

Avoid the temptation to be exact about how the prophecies will be fulfilled when studying the prophecies of the End Time. Seek a good understanding of the prophecies so that you can know when they are fulfilled. By following this format, it will be almost impossible for you to miss these sign posts that God has provided.

CHAPTER TWO

The When, Why and What of the End Times

At the mention of the term "end times," what come to the mind of most people are end-of-the-world events. Their thoughts race to events leading to the end of the world. This thinking is not what Scripture teaches. We are made to understand that this world will never end. It is written explicitly in the Bible:

> *"But Israel shall be saved in the Lord with an everlasting salvation: ye shall not be ashamed nor confounded world without end." (Isaiah 45:17)*

> *"Unto him be glory in the church by Christ Jesus throughout all ages, world without end. Amen."* (Ephesians 3:21)

The same Bible that tells us that this world has no end also says the world was destroyed by flood during the time of Noah.

> *"And God said unto Noah, the end of all flesh is come before me; for the earth is filled with violence through them; and, behold, I will destroy them with the earth."* (Genesis 6:13)

After the whole earth was covered with water for a period and all creatures outside of the ark, whether it be man or animal, were destroyed, the planet itself was not destroyed. Noah and his family, and all the animals that entered the ark, all came out and continued living on the earth.

> *"And every living substance was destroyed which was upon the face of the ground, both man, and cattle, and the creeping things, and the fowl of the heaven; and they were destroyed from the earth: and Noah only remained alive, and they that were with him in the ark."* (Genesis 7:23)

What does the Bible mean by the words "last days," "time of the end," and "latter days"? Let us visit places in the Bible where such words were used.

> *"And he said, go thy way, Daniel: for the words are closed up and sealed till the time of the end."* (Daniel 12:9)

"And it shall come to pass in the last days, that the mountain of the Lord's house shall be established in the top of the mountains and shall be exalted above the hills; and all nations shall flow unto it." (Isaiah 2:2)

"Afterward shall the children of Israel return, and seek the Lord their God, and David their king; and shall fear the Lord and his goodness in the latter days." (Hosea 3:5)

To the everyday person, the term "end times" paints the picture of an exploding world, a world being blown to smithereens by legions of explosives, or a world burning in unquenchable fire, but this isn't what the Bible means when it mentions "the time of the end."

What God's word means by these terms is the end of the world system and not the end of the planet itself. The ruler of the world system as it is currently structured is satan. We learned in the Scriptures that Jesus Christ is coming back again to this world to set up an earthly kingdom where He will rule as King and the devil will have no place there.

"And the devil that deceived them was cast into the lake of fire and brimstone, where the beast and the false prophet are, and shall be tormented day and night forever and ever" (Revelation 20:10)

"And I saw a new heaven and a new earth: for the first heaven and the first earth were passed away; and there was no more sea" (Revelation 21:1).

Therefore, End-Time refers to a time when an end will be put to the rule of satan, and Christ's rule will commence.

The wicked reign of the devil began in the Garden of Eden. It was there that he deceived Adam and his wife Eve. By choosing to believe the devil against God's truth, they gave satan rulership over their lives. They ate the forbidden fruit of the tree of the knowledge of good and evil and fell into sin. Since then, all of humanity has fallen into this sinful Adamic nature. All the pain and toil we struggle with can be traced back to this deception.

When Did It Start and When Will It End?

The End Time began at the cross when satan was stripped of his authority, and sin was defeated. The devil's influence was eliminated when the King of Glory, Jesus Christ shed His blood for the remission of our sins on the cross. We were freed from the penalty of sin, but its presence is still with us. The defeat of satan has not been finalized—that time is coming. The death of Christ on the cross bequeathed us the opportunity of choice. (God created all of us as moral agents with inbuilt freewill.) We can now choose to believe and accept Jesus Christ or continue believing the lies of satan.

The establishment of God's rule and the end of satan's control, which refers to the end times, began at the cross when Jesus gave His life for the benefit of humanity. It will officially end after the Millennial Reign of Christ. During Jesus's 1,000-year reign, satan will be bound in the bottomless pit for 1000 years.

The 1000 years is significant because it is considered one day. Adam lived 930 years; 70 years shy of one day. Methuselah lived 969 years. No one made a day with God. Jesus, as representative of mankind, will make the day.

> *"But, beloved, be not ignorant of this one thing, that one day is with the Lord as a thousand years, and a thousand years as one day"* (2 Peter 3:8)

After the final demise of satan, the old heaven and old earth will cease to be, and there will now be a New Heaven and a New Earth. Sin will no longer be present. The two old worlds will have been cleansed, but not destroyed, by fire.

> *"As therefore the tares are gathered and burned in the fire; so, shall it be in the end of this world"* (Matthew 13:40).

The term "end times" points to the end of satan's rule and the beginning of God's. Are you prepared for it?

CHAPTER THREE

Israel in the End Times

The most important sign of the End Times is the nation of Israel. Prophecies concerning Israel are the key to making sense of all that is happening and will soon occur in our world. There are more end-time prophecies about Israel than any other subject. In the End Time, Israel will no doubt be the main focal point for most, if not all, of the significant events that unfold before our very eyes before the King of Kings—the Christ of God— returns. End Time prophecies require the rebirth of the nation of Israel for any of the prophecies to be relevant.

For an exceptionally long time, the Jewish people were dispersed among the nations of the world. However, in 1948, they returned to their homeland of Israel in the Middle East as an independent nation. This single step became the indisputable signal that the End Time has indeed come upon us.

From the standpoint of God, Israel is re-gathered and returned to their land to be judged and eventually saved in the end. From the perspective of man, Israel as a nation will become the major trouble spots that will spearhead World War III.

The Key to End Time Prophecy

Virtually every generation, since the first coming of Christ, has had some individuals who believed that the End Time is at hand. The people who have heard the "end time is near" preaching's and teachings many times, do not seem to want to believe it, so these teachers only generate disbelief and disdain from their listeners. Therefore, anybody who dares to say we are living on the eve of destruction and annihilation runs the risk of automatic rejection from those who have heard the story too many times.

Why is it that for the people who have, for over 1900 years, attempted to predict the time of the Lord's coming, have not been correct? Despite all the confusion that has taken place in the past because of inaccurate interpretations or the overzealousness of some believers, God's word has left humankind with one specific sign that can ultimately settle and clear all uncertainties that concern the End Time. This single prophecy has the necessary ingredients of a sign so unique and so powerful that its fulfillment cannot be compared with any other condition. The Bible even makes us realize that the fulfillment of this one prophecy will be a conspicuous guide in the End Time for all to see. The occurrence of this event will be undeniable, and when it does happen, our world will have witnessed the event that will signal the end of the world. This single sign is the rebirth of Israel as a nation. On the 14th of May 1948, the ancient land of Israel was re-established as a nation. According to the word of God, this single event should warn us about the nearness of the End Time, more than any other events occurring in the world today.

Generations past could not point to Israel as a prophetic fulfillment because they have been scattered, for countless generations, among other nations of the earth. They have been without a homeland; endlessly persecuted and unwanted everywhere they journey. It makes biblical sense to say that the second coming of Christ would still be a thing of the future if the nation of Israel had not existed. The rebirth of Israel as a recognized nation, therefore, makes it a reality. For this reason, we can say that this generation has witnessed what is, without a doubt, the greatest miracle since the first time Christ walked this earth.

Bible predictions about the Jews/Israel as a nation are extraordinary. In this chapter, we will come to learn about how unique the Jewish people are among other nations on this earth, how God chose them to fulfill a purpose, how they sinned against God and abandoned Him, how God scattered them out of their land, how they lived many years outside their home, and how God finally brought them together.

The Scattering of Israel

The Roman Army, under the leadership of Pompey, entered Judea in 63 B.C. It did not take long before they reached the gates of Jerusalem. The fourth world empire with their massive forces, siege machines, and catapults quickly ran over the city of Jerusalem, and before long, the territory of Israel became another Roman Empire-controlled province.

The Jewish people, from the time of the Babylonian captivity forward, have continually existed within the territorial interests of other superior power. The land God promised Abraham and his descendants has for many years been a profitable asset for World Empires. As a result of this, the Jewish people have always hoped for a Messiah; someone who would free them from the back-breaking yoke of foreign domination. The Jewish people were so much in need of a savior that when Christ began His earthly ministry, they did not know and did not believe He was the Messiah. Their version of a Messiah was someone who would free them from the yoke of the Gentile rule and establish the Kingdom of God.

The son of the Emperor, Titus, in the year 70 A.D. led four Roman legions to the gate of Jerusalem. The aim was to quell a Jewish rebellion that began many years earlier. The walls of the city of Jerusalem were breached. The temple destroyed and burned, and many people killed. Titus gave the order that all the inhabitants of Jerusalem be taken captive and the city completely burned to the ground. The Jewish rebellion was finally squelched three years later in Masada.

By the time of Jesus Christ, the Roman Empire had successfully set up a firm and forceful government over the Jewish people. Herod the Great was the king then. He ruled over the Palestinian Province. It was he who spectacularly renovated the second temple after King Nebuchadnezzar of Babylon destroyed the first temple. King Herod also added many magnificent and breathtaking architectural structures to the city.

The book of Luke chapter 21 explicitly gives a detailed prediction about the destruction of Israel:

> *But when you see Jerusalem surrounded by armies, then know and understand that its desolation has come near.*

Then let those who are in Judea flee to the mountains, and let those who are inside [the city] get out of it, and let not those who are out in the country come into it;

For those are days of vengeance [of rendering full justice or satisfaction], that all things that are written may be fulfilled.

Alas for those who are pregnant and for those who have babies which they are nursing in those days! For great misery and anguish and distress shall be upon the land and indignation and punishment and retribution upon this people.

They will fall by [f]the mouth and the edge of the sword and will be led away as captives to and among all nations; and Jerusalem will be trodden down by the Gentiles until the times of the Gentiles are fulfilled (completed). (Luke 21:20-24 Amplified).

From the time of Christ Jesus forward, the Jewish people have experienced the cruelest wrath of God, even to the extent of God forsaking them. They have been dispersed to virtually every corner of the earth. They have been unwanted refugees in countless places. The Bible tells us that this situation will remain the same until the end of the age when He will finally put an end to all the Gentile world powers. In the book of Hosea, God stated how things would look for

the children of Israel before He finally comes to
redeem them:

> For the children of Israel shall dwell and sit deprived
> many days, without king or prince, without sacrifice or
> [idolatrous] pillar, and without ephod [a garment worn
> by priests when seeking divine counsel] or teraphim
> (household gods). (Hosea 3:4, Amplified)

Since 70 A.D. when Jerusalem was destroyed,
the above prophecy has been completely fulfilled,
even to the last dot. For centuries, the Jewish people
had no leader or king. God's chosen people made no
sacrifices because the temple was yet to be rebuilt
since the Romans last destroyed it. Just as Hosea
prophesied it, the Jewish people have been without a
form of temple worship and a homeland for nearly
2,000 years.

Restoration of the State of Israel

It was in 70 A.D. that the Roman Empire
destroyed Jerusalem and laid waste to their temple,
and then the Jews were dispersed all over the world.
As if that was not enough, Adolf Hitler's 1945 reign
of terror almost wiped them out and further scattered
them. The scattering of the Jewish people is a
fulfillment of an Old Testament prophecy. This
prophecy was a judgment upon them because of their
inability to obey God and follow His rules.

"And they shall fall by the edge of the sword and shall be led away captive into all nations: and Jerusalem shall be trodden down of the Gentiles, until the times of the Gentiles be fulfilled." (Luke 21:24)

God being the merciful Father that He is, says that He will still be their God and will continue to honor the original covenant He made with their forefathers—Abraham, Isaac, and Jacob. He said this after pronouncing judgment on them that they would fall by the sword and be led away captive, and that He would return them to their Promised Land before the Lord's second coming.

And I will bring again the captivity of my people of Israel, and they shall build the waste cities, and inhabit them; and they shall plant vineyards, and drink the wine thereof; they shall also make gardens and eat the fruit of them. And I will plant them upon their land, and they shall no more be pulled up out of their land which I have given them, saith the Lord thy God. (Amos 9:14-15)

And it shall come to pass in that day, that the Lord shall set his hand again the second time to recover the remnant of his people, which shall be left, from Assyria, and from Egypt, and from Pathros, and from Cush, and from Elam, and from Shinar, and from Hamath, and from the islands of the sea. And he shall set up an ensign for the nations, and shall assemble the outcasts of Israel, and gather together the dispersed of Judah from the four corners of the earth. (Isaiah 11:11-12)

This major event took place on the 14th of May 1948. After the Holocaust, Jewish people from all over the world began coming back to their homeland of Israel to re-establish it as their home state.

The analogy that Jesus used while talking about this was that of a fig tree. It is written in the Bible that the generation that witnesses the restoration of the Jewish people will not pass away before His return. Therefore, I say, The End is Not Near...It's Here. We do not know the time or the day, but we do know that it will come according to God's word.

Now learn a parable of the fig tree; When his branch is yet tender, and putteth forth leaves, ye know that summer is nigh: So likewise, ye, when ye shall see all these things, know that it is near, even at the doors. Verily I say unto you, this generation shall not pass, till all these things be fulfilled. (Matthew 24:32-34)

Although it is quite difficult to know the time frame that Jesus had in mind when He used the word "generation," which may mean 100 years or less, whatever the time maybe, those signs indicate that the time is almost upon us.

Jerusalem the Capital of Israel

Since the 70 A.D. destruction of Jerusalem by the Roman Empire, the city has moved from one power to another. It moved from the Roman conquerors to the Persians, from there to the crusaders, then the Turks, to the British, and back to the real owners in the 1967 popular "6-day war." For the first time in several centuries, the Jewish people assumed control of their favorite city.

> *And they shall fall by the edge of the sword and shall be led away captive into all nations: and Jerusalem shall be trodden down of the Gentiles, until the times of the Gentiles be fulfilled.* (Luke 21:24)

It is widely believed among Bible scholars that the Antichrist will make a peace treaty with Israel at the beginning of the Great Tribulation period in something that concerns the rebuilding of the Jewish temple. It is strongly believed that midway through this period and after this individual has been accepted, he will make an image of himself, declare himself God and demand worship for himself and his image.

> *That ye be not soon shaken in mind, or be troubled, neither by spirit, nor by word, nor by letter as from us, as that the day of Christ is at hand. Let no man deceive you by any means: for that day shall not come, except there come a falling away first, and that man of sin be*

revealed, the son of perdition; Who opposeth and exalteth himself above all that is called God, or that is worshipped; so that he as God sitteth in the temple of God, shewing himself that he is God. (2 Thessalonians 2:2-4)

The Jewish people will refuse his proposal and reject his person. This act will bring severe persecution upon the Jews. All this is to happen in Jerusalem, the capital of the state of Israel. For this prophecy to be fulfilled, Israel must become a sovereign nation. I was born in 1947, one year before Israel was reborn as a nation following the 1948 Arab–Israeli War.

After enlisting in the military, I was stationed in Seoul, Korea, in 1967. Shortly after arriving there we were told that the Arab and Israeli military forces had begun what we now call the Six-Day War in the Middle East. Israel prevailed as the victor, but the battle of land and control persist to this day between Israeli and the Arab states. During the war in 1967, Israel took possession of over two-thirds of the Golan Heights amongst other territories while the Arab countries kept the remaining one-third. Israel's control and sovereign rights over this territory have been a debate with previous U.S. administrations siding with the United Nations that Israel should relinquish their control and claim to Golan Heights back to the Arab states. Previous administrations have not been able to broker a deal with Israeli and

Arab officials. President Trump has added works to his faith in Jerusalem via his actions, which are signs of God using this unconventional candidate to propel His will.

(1) President Trump not only acknowledges Jerusalem as Israel's capital.

(2) President Trump sided with Israel's control of the Golan Heights by endorsing their sovereignty over the area. (See also the map from the US Library of Congress showing the Golan Heights as "Israeli Occupied.")

(3) President Trump backed up his conviction by being the first U.S. President to begin the process to have the U.S. Embassy for Israel moved from Tel Aviv to Jerusalem.

I am not talking about these things to get into politics. Instead, I say these truths to show you how the things that are played out in the headlines today were prophesied in the Bible and are the steppingstones to what will come as the end ushers into fruition right before our very eyes. Presidents Trump's validation of Jerusalem as headquarters paves the way for the fulfillment of scriptures. Jesus is coming back to Jerusalem.

Mr. Donald Trump is doing what no one else was able or willing to do because of his appointed time.

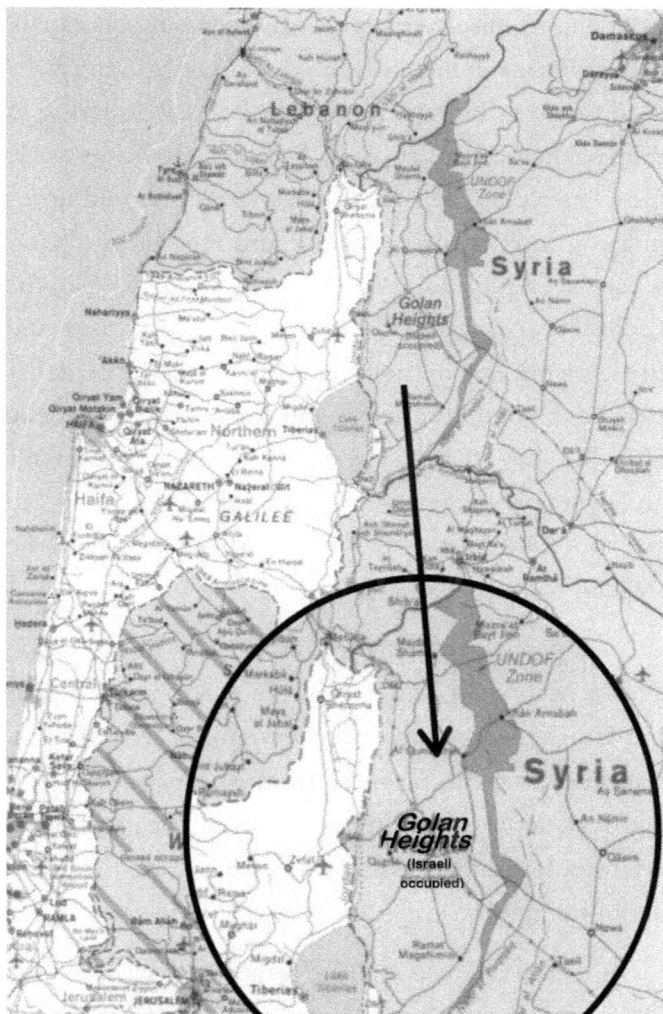

Figure 2 Map: Enhanced map from US LOC showing "Israeli occupied" Golan Heights.

Source: United States Central Intelligence Agency. *Israel*. [Washington, D.C.: Central Intelligence Agency, 1988] Map. Retrieved from the Library of Congress, <www.loc.gov/item/2005631060/>

God had to raise someone with unyielding chutzpah! I think it took someone as bold and unorthodox as he is to do what he has done. All of this is ushering in things that God has spoken. As I said, God uses us all. God has a plan, and He uses us all. We should never judge a book by its cover because regardless if God wants to employ someone, He will. God will take the foolish to confound the wise. Just like Moses and those mentioned in the Bible. Just like all the preacher that have gone before me and those who will come after me. Just like the President of the United States and every person birth into this world. God has a plan for you. God knew what your purpose was when he formed you.

On Wednesday the 6th of December 2017, President Donald Trump gave the announcement that the United States now fully recognizes Jerusalem as Israel's capital and he also gave the order for the U.S. Embassy to be moved from its current location in Tel Aviv to Jerusalem. For decades, America has been about doing this.

The 6-day war of 1967 gave the Jewish people total control over Jerusalem. In 1980, Israel gave a proclamation that the city of Jerusalem would be united as its capital forever. Jerusalem has since then been the location of the Supreme Court, the office of the Prime Minister, and other government offices. It has also been the command center of Israel's Parliament known as the Knesset. What the United States is doing is recognizing the long-standing fact that Jerusalem has been Israel's seat of government for many years now.

Nevertheless, this is a very controversial move because the people of Palestine are also bent on establishing their capital in East Jerusalem. Many of the Muslim nations have severely warned that the action taken by the U.S. government could lead to unrest in the region. Abbas, President of Palestine, said the move would ultimately end any chance for peace with Israel. The President of Turkey, Recep Tayyip Erdoğan, said these events might lead to severing the bilateral relations his country has with Israel. The President of Turkey, Recep Tayyip Erdoğan, said these events may lead to severing the bilateral relations his country has with Israel. Islamic terrorist groups like Hamas are calling for a region-wide protest. It is even likely that terror attacks may be carried out as a reprisal to Trump's statement.

As huge as this move is for the United States, it is also an incredibly significant event in the calendar of End Time prophecy. According to the Bible, Israel will be in their land and control Jerusalem before the occurrence of the major events of the End Time. In addition,

Prophet Zechariah prophesied that, during the final wars, all nations will wage war against Jerusalem:

> *For I will gather all nations against Jerusalem to battle, and the city shall be taken and the houses rifled and the women ravished; and half of the city shall go into exile, but the rest of the people shall not be cut off from the city.* (Zechariah 14:2)

The prophet also prophesied that the city of Jerusalem would be the most dangerous place on earth, and all the nations of the earth will come together against it.

> *Behold, I am about to make Jerusalem a cup or bowl of reeling to all the peoples round about, and in the siege against Jerusalem will there also be a siege against and upon Judah.*
>
> *And in that day, I will make Jerusalem a burdensome stone for all peoples; all who lift it or burden themselves with it shall be sorely wounded. And all the nations of the earth shall come and gather together against it.* (Zechariah 12:2-3)

Before now, there was tension in the Middle East primarily against the nation of Israel and directly against the city Jerusalem, just like it was prophesied in the Bible. The tension has exponentially gone up now that President Trump has recognized Jerusalem as the capital of Israel. It will not be long before this snowballing conflict threatens the whole world with war!

These signs and many others have been fulfilled in our lifetime. We are truly living in the End Time.

CHAPTER FOUR

Israel and the Temple

The Rebuilding of the Temple

Even with winning the 6-day war of 1967, which brought the control of Jerusalem under the Jewish people, the Temple Mount could not be recovered. The Temple Mount is supposed to be the site of the Holy Temple.

How did it happen? The Jewish people initially took control of this mount because of the 1967 war, but for some political reasons, they relinquished control back to the Muslims. One of their aims was to show tolerance for other religions. As you are reading this book, there is a Muslim mosque called the Dome of the Rock on this site.

From all indication, it is quite clear that the Muslims do not have any plans of handing over the mount or removing their mosque, anytime soon. And for all the prophecies that the Scriptures gave to be fulfilled, this temple must be built.

> *When ye therefore shall see the abomination of desolation, spoken of by Daniel the prophet, stand in the holy place, (whoso readeth, let him understand.* (Matthew 24:15)

The Jewish people have already made plans as to how the temple will be built when they get the chance. It will only take the Jewish people two years to build it when the Lord supernaturally makes it possible.

King Solomon built the first temple. This temple was destroyed in 586 B.C. It was rebuilt a second time in 26 B.C. and later dissolved in 70 A.D. by the Romans.

> *And it came to pass in the four hundred and eightieth year after the children of Israel were come out of the land of Egypt, in the fourth year of Solomon's reign over Israel, in the month Zif, which is the second month, that he began to build the house of the Lord.* (1 Kings 6:1)

It seems that when the time comes, the Beast will play a critical role in the rebuilding of the temple. He may be the one who sets up a peace treaty that will lead to the actualization of this prophecy. While the building of the temple is ongoing, his peace treaty will be intact. Once it is completed and we are at the end of the first three and a half years, the Antichrist will break this treaty with Israel, set himself in the temple, and proclaim himself God. This is probably when the second half of the tribulation will start, leading to the greatest persecution and death the Christian and Jewish community has ever experienced. It will be pure misery.

The Beast will take the life of 2/3 of the Jewish people. This persecution will be worse and far deadlier than the German Holocaust that took 6 million Jews' lives.

> *And it shall come to pass, that in all the land, saith the Lord, two parts therein shall be cut off and die; but the third shall be left therein. And I will bring the third part through the fire, and will refine them as silver is refined, and will try them as gold is tried: they shall call on my name, and I will hear them: I will say, It is my people: and they shall say, The Lord is my God.* (Zechariah 13:8-9)

The temple must be rebuilt for the Abomination of Desolation to take place. It will also serve as a critical time in the End Time events that will let the rest of the world know that TIME IS UP!

Trump and the Temple

In the wake of the statement made by President Donald Trump to move the American Embassy from Tel Aviv to Jerusalem, much backlash occurred. As

Christians, we support his declaration because we understand the significance of Jerusalem being the capital of Israel. It is safe to say that Mr. Trump has a role to play in the rebuilding of the temple.

Aljazeera, a Muslim news network is worried that Israel may become increasingly bold because of Trump's recognition of Jerusalem. Aljazeera also wondered about the probability of this recognition leading to the building of Temple. The prophecies in the Bible concerning the building of the Temple and the End Times are top of mind for Aljazeera viewers. This demonstrates that even those who are not traditional Christians are giving audience to the Signs of the Times.

David Sheen, a Jewish journalist, tweeted about the possibility of President Trump being the one that will propose the Temple's rebuilding. His tweet showed Donald Trump, in a cartoon, visiting the Temple Mount, and seeing the perfect location for the reconstruction of the temple. Like I said earlier, who would be better to get this Temple rebuilt than Trump or a world leader in the ranks of Trump?

A New Religious Court

A rabbinical organization that dissolved nearly 1600 years ago is now operating in Israel. This group of senior rabbis is known as the *Sanhedrin*, whose job is to reinstitute the full worship practices of Judaism as was practiced in the Old Testament. This religious group was formally one of Israel's principal forces in both religion and politics. The Sanhedrin is a seventy-one council of Jewish sages who, during the time of the Romans in Judea, constituted the legislative body and the Supreme Court. To the Jews in Israel, this group represented their supreme religious governing body even when they were under foreign powers.

Members of this organization performed the functions of governing the people, controlling worship upon the Temple mount, and functioning as judges of a high court. These people were behind the trial, condemnation, and crucifixion of Christ Jesus in 32 A.D. The destruction of the Temple in 70 A.D. and the scattering of the Jewish people that happened afterward resulted in the Sanhedrin losing its function and authority.

However, the Sanhedrin tried to hold together for many centuries after the Temple and Jerusalem were destroyed, but having no real purpose, they later disbanded in 425 A.D. For many centuries after, the Sanhedrin only existed in memories until recent times. Now that the nation of Israel is back in their land, it is now time for the reinstitution of the sacred worship practices of Judaism. Israel's growing religious movements led to the re-establishment of the Sanhedrin council in 2004.

The re-establishment of the Sanhedrin in our generation is another sign that the fulfillment of End Time prophecies is coming to pass. The Sanhedrin is currently structured as it was in the first century times: composed of over 70 rabbis. Their focus is the re-establishment of the Jewish state to how it functioned during the Second Temple era. This will primarily transform the nation of Israel from the secular one that it is to a more religious state. Another of their focus is the rebuilding of the Temple, which will be the major focal point for the sacrifices and worship, as stated in the Torah.

The events that surround the movement for the rebuilding of the Temple and the re-establishment of the Sanhedrin council further lend credence to the fact that the nation of Israel has a big role to play in the fulfillment of End Time prophecy. Two great requirements for the fulfillment of many of the important events of the End Time prophecy are the rebuilding of the Temple and the establishment of a functioning Levitical priesthood, and both seem to be on track.

Jewish Priests Relearning Temple Worship

In preparation for the rebuilding of the Jerusalem Temple Mount, Israel's Levitical priests are now relearning the laws and traditions associated with Temple worship as was initially prescribed by Moses. Since the 70 A.D. Roman destruction of the Temple, the Jews have not practiced these traditions. This is because there was no central worship place to carry them out, and the subsequent scattering did not help the matter.

In recent months, full dress reenactments for the original daily Tamid service, the Passover offering, the water libation, the First Fruits, the Shavuot, many other special Temple services, including all the annual feast day celebrations of the Jewish people have taken place. Knowing fully well that these traditions have not been practiced for centuries, the Temple Institute, therefore, set up training classes to teach the Kohanim (priests) the precise way to carry out each Temple activity.

The priests are preparing for the glorious day of the dedication of the Jerusalem Temple mount. That day appears to be coming quickly, by all estimates. The Temple must be rebuilt just as it has been prophesied for the fulfillment of the prophecy on its desecration by the Antichrist near the middle of the last seven years. The Antichrist will, in the act of ultimate defiance against the Almighty God, stop the worship and sacrifices of the Temple and then proclaim himself God. This is what is known as the Abomination of Desolation. There are other biblical prophecies, according to the Bible passages below, that predict the Lord's return on the rebuilding of the Temple, as He's to come down upon the Mount of Olives in glory and enter the Temple via the East gate.

> *And when He had said this, even as they were looking [at Him], He was caught up, and a cloud received and carried Him away out of their sight.*

> *And while they were gazing intently into heaven as He went, behold, two men [dressed] in white robes suddenly stood beside them,*

> *Who said, Men of Galilee, why do you stand gazing into heaven? This same Jesus, who was caught away and lifted up from among you into heaven, will return in [just] the same way in which you saw Him go into heaven.*

> *Then [the disciples] went back to Jerusalem from the hill called Olivet, which is near Jerusalem, [only] a Sabbath day's journey (three-quarters of a mile) away.* (Acts 1:9-12)

> *AFTERWARD, the man [an angel] brought me to the gate, the gate that faces east.*

And behold, the glory of the God of Israel came from the east and His voice was like the sound of many waters, and the earth shone with His glory.

And the vision which I saw was like the vision I had seen when I came to foretell the destruction of the city and like the vision, I had seen beside the river Chebar [near Babylon]; and I fell on my face.

And the glory of the Lord entered the temple by the gate facing east. (Ezekiel 43:1-4)

The Jewish people passionately believe that their place of worship in the Jerusalem Temple mount will soon be built. The Levitical priests are seriously getting ready for that day. The preparation for this day necessitated the training of the Levites on how to properly conduct worship after close to 2,000 years of its neglect.

The Jerusalem Temple Mount, when rebuilt, will be a substantial prophetic fulfillment. It will set things rolling for the actualization of the prophecies concerning the last seven years before the coming of Christ. It will also finally signal to all that End Time events are indeed upon us. We are getting closer to the day the Son of Man will return in His power and glory!

CHAPTER FIVE

The Nations Turn Against Israel

With Trump's adoption of Jerusalem as Israel's capital, a dramatic shift is beginning to occur in global politics. The massive Hezbollah-inspired protest involving tens of thousands of Lebanese and Palestinians, public outcries from world leaders, and the passage of the UN Resolution 2334 by the United Nations Security Council on Dec. 23, 2016, are signs that things are taking a new and dangerous turn, and the world is entering into an even more dangerous period. Considering the way things are shaping up, we are entering a period where all nations of the world will turn against Israel both politically and militarily. Unknown to a lot of people who crave for peace in the Middle East, these events are powerful precursors of what is written in the Bible concerning the End Time.

Before the coming to power of President Trump, the Administration of President Obama took an anti-Israel stand. They took calculated action against Israel and condemned Israel on settlements and even abstained in a Security Council vote, something the U.S always vetoes. It was like there's a behind-the-scene plan and effort to frustrate, isolate, and destroy Israel. Using the words of the former Speaker of the United States House of Representatives, Newt Gingrich, President Trump is to "prepare a comprehensive offensive…to undo the damage to Israel the Obama team is inflicting." It seems that this is exactly what Trump has been doing.

The Bible Predicted it

These events may look like the continuation of what has always been a tensed political situation in the Middle East, but there is more to these troubling events than what the ordinary mind can decipher. The Bible gives details of a series of amazing prophecies concerning Israel and the End Time. It is through the prism of these prophecies that we can better understand what has happened to Israel, what is happening to her right now, and what will still happen to her. These prophecies are in the best position to tell us the truth behind all the stories in the news, and where we are heading as we move closer towards the

End Time. By understanding these prophecies, we will now know why the present UN resolution and many other peace deals that may come after are sure to fail.

The prophecies of Prophet Joel give details about the restoration of the fortunes of Judah and Jerusalem at the end of the age. Even though these people have for long been scattered among other nations of the world, according as the Lord has spoken, they came back to their land and then formed a new nation.

> FOR BEHOLD, in those days and at that time when I shall reverse the captivity and restore the fortunes of Judah and Jerusalem,
>
> I will gather all nations and will bring them down into the Valley of Jehoshaphat, and there will I deal with and execute judgment upon them for [their treatment of] My people and of My heritage Israel, whom they have scattered among the nations and [because] they have divided My land. (Joel 3:1-2)

The prophecies talk about the Lord judging all the nations within the same general time that Israel returns to their land. This battle is prophesied to take place in the Valley of Armageddon coined from "Har Megiddo," meaning the Mount of Megiddo, in the ancient city of Megiddo.

The Bible tells us that this northern point of entry, in the End Time, will be the main route of the armies of the world in their fight against Israel. The armies will gather in the Valley of Armageddon. Hundreds of millions of people will gather in this valley for the final battle.

> *Then the sixth [angel] emptied his bowl on the mighty river Euphrates, and its water was dried up to make ready a road for [the coming of] the kings of the east (from the rising sun).*
>
> *And I saw three loathsome spirits like frogs, [leaping] from the mouth of the dragon and from the mouth of the beast and from the mouth of the false prophet.*
>
> *For really, they are the spirits of demons that perform signs (wonders, miracles). And they go forth to the rulers and leaders all over the world, to gather them together for war on the great day of God the Almighty.*
>
> *Behold, I am going to come like a thief! Blessed (happy, [a]to be envied) is he who stays awake (alert) and who guards his clothes, so that he may not be naked and [have the shame of being] seen exposed!*
>
> *And they gathered them together at the place which in Hebrew is called Armageddon.* (Revelation 16:12-16)

The Bible, according to Zechariah 12:1-3, predicts that the period before the final battle will be one of great distress.

> *THE BURDEN or oracle (the thing to be lifted up) of the word of the Lord concerning Israel: Thus, says the Lord, who stretches out the heavens and lays the foundation of the earth and forms the spirit of man within him:*
>
> *Behold, I am about to make Jerusalem a cup or bowl of reeling to all the peoples round about, and in the siege against Jerusalem will there also be a siege against and upon Judah.*
>
> *And in that day, I will make Jerusalem a burdensome stone for all peoples; all who lift it or burden themselves with it shall be sorely wounded. And all the nations of the earth shall come and gather together against it.*

According to the prophecy, Judah and Jerusalem will be the center of great hatred and fear in the End Time. Jerusalem will become a burdensome stone for all peoples. The growing tension between Arabs and the Jews will reach a dangerous point where all nations will greatly fear what will come out of it. This tension is getting worse as the UN and many other nations are condemning Israel for settling in Jerusalem and Judea.

Eventually, whatever resolution the UN enacts (even if it is the declaration of a separate Palestinian state) or whatever diplomacy is attempted, it will fail badly, and the tensions will result in a massive war in the Middle East. It is predicted that this war will begin by an attack that will come from Israel's old enemies, Egypt, and Syria, according to Prophet Daniel.

> *And at the time of the end the king of the South shall push at and attack him, and the king of the North shall come against him like a whirlwind, with chariots and horsemen and with many ships; and he shall enter into the countries and shall overflow and pass through.* (Daniel 11:40)

This initial war will, in no time, increase exponentially as other nations join the war, leading to a terrifying global war. This is World War III. According to Prophet Ezekiel, the nation of Russia and her allies will attack Israel in the battle of Gog and Magog, as detailed in Ezekiel chapter 38 and 39.

Explaining Ezekiel chapter 38 and 39, Gog represents world leaders that are in opposition against God. Meshech and Tubal are the same as Moschi and Tibareni, the Greek tribes. Rosh is the same as Russia. The death toll of the war will be in the millions.

These events will mark the start of the Great Tribulation and will lead to the destruction of the whole world. The biblical predictions of war and destruction on a global scale are why the city of

Jerusalem is today turning into a burdensome stone for all people.

This is coming at a time when Israel's religious groups are advocating that the Jewish Temple be rebuilt on the mount. Can you imagine the level of tensions these events will generate in the Middle East when it happens?

CHAPTER SIX

Alternative Lifestyles

Everywhere we turn, the signs are there that we are in the End Time. We live in a time when the world openly embraces and celebrates sexual immorality. Christians who try to stand firm and follow Christ are mocked at the slightest opportunity. Programs and events that promote and celebrate sexual permissiveness, adultery, fornication, and alternative lifestyles are daily aired and hosted. We now applaud people who do ungodly and unnatural things.

We are now in the time of Noah

And as it was in the days of Noah, so shall it be also in the days of the Son of man. They did eat, they drank, they married wives, they were given in marriage, until the day that Noah entered into the ark, and the flood came, and destroyed them all. (Luke 17:26-27)

Let us ask ourselves the question, what was it like in the days of Noah and Lot? By checking some Bible verses, we will learn how things were then. Luke 17:28-30 makes us know that in Lot's day, the people were busy "eating and drinking" to celebrate what can now be described as the general adoption and legalization of alternative lifestyles.

> *So also [it was the same] as it was in the days of Lot. [People] ate, they drank, they bought, they sold, they planted, they built; but on the [very] day that Lot went out of Sodom, it rained fire and brimstone from heaven and destroyed [them] all. That is the way it will be on the day that the Son of Man is revealed.*

In Jude 1:7, the Bible says that the people of Sodom and Gomorrah in the day of Lot gave themselves over to impurity and indulged in unnatural vice and sensual perversion. So, in the day of Noah, people celebrated alternative lifestyles as a normal lifestyle while in Lot's day, it was indulging in unnatural vice. This will be how things will look in the End Time and before the return of Christ.

> *[The wicked are sentenced to suffer] just as Sodom and Gomorrah and the adjacent towns--which likewise gave themselves over to impurity and indulged in unnatural vice and sensual perversity—are laid out [in plain sight]*

as an exhibit of perpetual punishment [to warn] of everlasting fire.

Not only do we have our streets and homes littered with sexual immorality, but gay sex is also now a norm. Nothing less than 14 countries, since 2001, have openly and fully legalized homosexual (same sex) marriage. Countries like Canada, Argentina, Belgium, Denmark, Norway, Iceland, Netherlands, Portugal, South Africa, Spain, Sweden, Uruguay, New Zealand, France, America, and Mexico have joined the train. This list is continually growing.

The truth is that the issue of alternative lifestyles did not start today, it has been around for a long time, but it has never been this embraced, flaunted, and celebrated by society. Now wedding songs are being written, and cakes are being baked for homosexual marriage. The legalization of gay marriage is at a greater level of acceptance, and it is a sign that we are close to the End Time. It will most likely be the final straw that leads to the end of all mankind.

Alternative lifestyles may be considered a normal thing in our world today, but God still sees it as a wicked act, and Jesus says it is one of the End Time signs. No matter how the devil and his angels dress it up to make it look like a normal alternative lifestyle for people, the Bible still says, it is an abomination. Of course, some may think or even argue that gay marriage is not a sign that will predict a signal of when Christ will return. One thing you should know is that Jesus tells us it will be one of the signs according to Matthew 24:37, which says, *"As were the days of Noah, so will be the coming of the Son of Man."*

In December 2017, Australia expanded the list of countries that had legalized gay marriage. This abominable list began with the Netherlands in December of 2000 and more countries have joined. Most of them are in Europe and the Americas.

Gay rights activists and advocates are not only turning the world into Sodom and Gomorrah, but they are also leading the world on the path of destruction. Homosexual sins greatly precipitated the arrival of the Great Flood that destroyed the world in the time of Noah. The sin of alternative lifestyles forced the hand of God to send the flood.

Alternative Lifestyles and Antichrist

The way gay rights activists and advocates are attacking and destroying our freedom and human rights will most likely be the format the coming Antichrist will employ. The way Christians are being persecuted and even forced to embrace and celebrate alternative lifestyles will clear the path for the dictatorial future world leader.

Do not be surprised that when the Antichrist comes, it will look any different than the way the LGBT-inclusive non-discrimination laws are being used to persecute Christians. The Antichrist will most likely behead, imprison, and grossly persecute Christians on issues like alternative lifestyles. People will be forced to embrace and celebrate it; the same way people are being forced to employ and bake cakes for them. By allowing this abominable practice to go on, mankind has opened the way for greater evil to befall them.

Alternative Lifestyles and What the People Think

The buildup to the Supreme Court's ruling on Obergefell v. Hodges got a lot of people greatly worried, but when it was finally announced on June 26, 2015, that same-sex marriage was now legal in the US, people grew more concerned and alarmed about the nearness of the End Time. According to a published data by Bible Gateway, searches on their website BibleGateway.com climbed exponentially, peaking on the 29th of June. After the same-sex legalization decision of the Supreme Court, many people went on this site to conduct searches in their attempt at finding the relation between this same-sex marriage decision and End Time events. The keywords for the searches were *end times.* The searches were more than 5 times the average daily searches on the site. This is to tell you that ordinary people can even see the relation between alternative lifestyles and the End Time.

> *You shall not lie with a man as with a woman; it is an abomination.* (Leviticus 18:22)

The continual and unabated rise of alternative lifestyles is critical evidence of a society that has abandoned God and departed from His teachings that are clearly against such practice. It is a detestable and abominable act in the sight of God for same sex to have sexual relations.

Countries of the whole world seem to be rushing and falling over themselves to legalize same-sex marriage. They no longer care about what God's word says.

This is what God thinks of same-sex union legalization:

> *Now we recognize and know that the Law is good if anyone uses it lawfully [for the purpose for which it was designed],*
>
> *Knowing and understanding this: that the Law is not enacted for the righteous (the upright and just, who are*

in right standing with God), but for the lawless and unruly, for the ungodly and sinful, for the irreverent and profane, for those who strike and beat and [even] murder fathers and strike and beat and [even] murder mothers, for manslayers,

[For] impure and immoral persons, those who abuse themselves with men, kidnappers, liars, perjurers--and whatever else is opposed to wholesome teaching and sound doctrine. (1 Timothy 1:8–10)

Around fifteen of the countries that have given the nod for same-sex union are from Europe, a continent believed to have been the focal point of revivals and worldwide evangelism. After the Netherlands in 2000, we have now had Belgium, Spain, Norway, Sweden, Iceland, Portugal, Denmark and now France. Twenty-six countries have made same-sex union laws, and the list is still expanding.

There are currently more than 100 million cases of diseases transmitted through sex, with 20 million new cases being yearly recorded in the United States alone. Also, in England, there have been large rises in STDs since 2012 (England happened to have legalized this type of union in 2013).

For this cause God gave them up unto vile affections: for even their women did change the natural use into that which is against nature: And likewise also the men, leaving the natural use of the woman, burned in their lust one toward another; men with men working that which is unseemly, and receiving in themselves that recompence of their error which was meet.

And even as they did not like to retain God in their knowledge, God gave them over to a reprobate mind, to do those things which are not convenient; Being filled with all unrighteousness, fornication, wickedness, covetousness, maliciousness; full of envy, murder, debate, deceit, malignity; whisperers, Backbiters, haters of God, despiteful, proud, boasters, inventors of evil things, disobedient to parents, Without understanding, covenantbreakers, without natural affection, implacable, unmerciful: Who knowing the judgment of God, that they which commit such things are worthy of death, not only do the same, but have pleasure in them that do them. (Romans 1:26-32)

Transgenderism and alternative lifestyles are the new anthems. We are daily inundated with messages of the gay lifestyle. The media, advocacy groups, governments, and NGOs are continually trying to force it down our throat. We see this obscene lifestyle almost everywhere, and it is slowly being intermingled into our society as something normal and acceptable, even though it is and will always be abominable in the sight of God.

Our world of today is oozing with all manners of sexual immorality. Check your television, and you will see alternative lifestyles, fornication, and adultery everywhere.

We are told in the book of Jude 1:7 that we should use the case of Sodom and Gomorrah as an example and escape the punishment God meted to them. His punishment for their sins, which also included alternative lifestyles, was destruction by fire. Destruction is what awaits us if we fail to heed His warning.

> *[The wicked are sentenced to suffer] just as Sodom and Gomorrah and the adjacent towns--which likewise gave themselves over to impurity and indulged in unnatural vice and sensual perversity—are laid out [in plain sight] as an exhibit of perpetual punishment [to warn] of everlasting fire.*

CHAPTER SEVEN

Natural Disasters

We are all aware of the global problems that our world has and is still experiencing, particularly in recent years; global warming, climate change, floods, earthquakes, etc. These are just a few of them. The thing is this: natural disaster incidents have rapidly grown over the last two decades. For those who closely follow current events and compare them with both history and Bible prophecies, they understand that this is not mere coincidence. The only problem with this type of prediction is that some religious fanatics and kooks always use the opportunity of any natural disaster to sing their "end time" songs.

Many prophets of doom have been doing this for long. For whatever reason they might have, they peddle their false news and narratives by capitalizing on people's fear. They move their theories from aliens to UFOs to natural and man-made disasters, and to any other kooky ideas they can find, thereby making it hard for genuine truth-seeker to be taken seriously.

Disasters have escalated on the earth, and volcanoes are blowing up around the globe. Earthquakes are happening throughout the world. Distress is in every nation with various perplexities. It is a fact, and there are statistics to prove it, that cases of natural disasters have greatly risen for the past 20 years or so. There must be a reason and an explanation for this.

Two-Fold Increase

From 1950 to 1990, the United States experienced classified cases of 142 natural disasters. Between 1990 and the year 2000, the number was 72. The next 9 years of 2000 to 2009 was the period when some of the most destructive and worse natural disasters in the history of man occurred all around the world. Of all these natural disasters, earthquakes have been the most destructive in terms of loss of property and life.

After earthquakes, storms at 22 percent and extreme temperatures at 11 percent have been recorded to be the deadliest natural disasters between 2000 and 2009. Results from the Secretariat press release of the United Nations International Strategy for Disaster

Reduction have shown that since the 1980 - 1989, catastrophic events have more than doubled.

The figures released by the Center for Research on Epidemiology of Disasters (CRED) in the year 2010 in Geneva shows that in just one decade, nearly 4,000 disasters have occurred and led to the death of nearly 800,000 people and, in one way or another, affected more than two billion others with cost of nearly $1 trillion.

Since the beginning of our current decade, we have seen signs of this trend continuing—from monumentally devastating earthquakes in Haiti, Turkey, and Chile, to record-shattering winter storms in North America and Europe. These disasters have resulted in the deaths of many, left many homeless, and greatly destroyed infrastructures of towns and cities.

> ...and there shall be earthquakes in divers' places, and there shall be famines and troubles: these are the beginnings of sorrows. (Mark 13:8)

The seas and waves are roaring. People are being wiped out in their thousands by floods and Tsunamis, and mankind is constantly asking the question, what is happening to our world? In the year 2010, the number of Federal Disaster Declarations in that year stood at a staggering 81. That was a new record. One year later, 2011 to be precise, the number shot to 99, breaking the former record. That year's disasters cost the American government a whopping 32 Billion Dollars. In 2012, the number of Disaster Declarations was higher than the previous year. The report shows that disaster declarations in the U.S. have been upward trending for the past 15 years.

In 2012, more than 32 million people were displaced because of natural disasters.

> *BUT UNDERSTAND this, that in the last days will come (set in) perilous times of great stress and trouble [hard to deal with and hard to bear].* (2 Timothy 3:1)

Tornadoes

The tornado that happened in Moore, Oklahoma in 2013 left nothing but a pile of rubble where apartments once stood. It was a massive EF4 twister with packing wind speeds of nearly 200 miles per hour that ransacked and laid waste to a U.S. town of 55,000 people. It led to the loss of 24 lives, leveled 2 schools, demolished many houses, and left many injured. Other states apart from Oklahoma have been hit by tornados. In May of the same year, Louisiana, Texas, Kansas, and Alabama were also hit.

Extreme Weather

There were records of many all-time low temperatures in this same 2013:

Bangladesh experienced their lowest temperature, since their 1971 independence, on the 10th of January 2013.

In China, they also faced what happened to be their coldest in 28 years.

Salt Lake City, Utah experienced their coldest since 1949.

India also experienced a very cold winter, the same with Northern Israel, Jerusalem, and Tel Aviv. The Middle East's extremely low temperature led to 17 deaths. In the same year, France, Russia, Hungary, Ukraine, Finland, and other countries equally experienced extreme weather events.

Hurricanes

After Hurricane Harvey, which set a record as the costliest natural disaster in the history of America, almost wiped out Houston, Texas, another Hurricane Irma hit Florida and Caribbean. This Hurricane was one of the biggest in the Atlantic Ocean. It was not long when another, Hurricane Maria, heavily descended on Puerto Rico, cutting off the power supply to the whole island.

Wildfires

Dozens of wildfires raged across the Pacific Northwest. These wildfires released a blanket of black smoke from the cascades with ash raining down on people, cars, and streets. It was so bad that the Governor of Washington declared a state of emergency.

People are saying that such an occurrence is nothing like what they have ever experienced. Meteorologists are surprised for the dry summer in places popularly known for their rainy climate.

Places near the Idaho and Oregon borders were shrouded in heavy smoke from wildfires in Oregon.

The Chetco Bar Fire in Oregon burned down nearly 175,000 acres of wilderness. The Eagle Creek Fire in Portland burned down nearly 30,000 acres. For the Diamond Creek Fire, it was close to 105,000 acres of land in North Central Washington and even crossing into Canada. The Norse Peak Fire burned nearly 45,000 acres near Mount Rainier.

Eclipse

For the first time in like 1,000 years, a part of the U.S. experienced a total eclipse from coast to coast.

Droughts

The world's freshwater supply is drying up. A drought of biblical proportions is taken place all over the world. Gigantic reservoirs, lakes, aquifers, and rivers are drying up fast. It is at an alarming rate that freshwater needed for bathing, cleaning, irrigation, and drinking is being depleted.

The 2014 California drought in the San Bernardino National Forest killed up to 15 million trees. It was so bad that it was predicted that many more trees will die the next year. As measured by the United States Drought Monitor, 93 percent of the State of California experienced this extreme, severe, and exceptional drought. Residents agreed that it was the state's drought of the century; something beyond what their parents or grandparents have ever experienced.

Disease Outbreak

After the Ebola epidemic that led to many deaths has been neutralized, another pathogenic virus rampaged the heartland of America. It was a very catastrophic bird flu outbreak that killed millions of birds in California, Arkansas, Idaho, and Iowa.

Sea Creatures

The extreme winter of 2013 was thought to be the worst for sea creatures known as sea lions, but the ghastly 2015 winter incidence led to the death of many of these creatures. It was estimated that the number of deaths was twice that of 2015. These lions were washed up, starved, and stranded on the shores of Southern California.

NGOs, government agencies, news media, and individuals blamed the unfortunate incidence on several strange events like weak ocean winds, abnormal food shortages, and warm coastal waters. Whatever may be responsible for those deaths, what is clear to even the deaf is that something unprecedented and strange is changing the position, arrangement, or order of the normal flow of our ecosystem, and the intensity is growing.

Why the Increase?

There was clearly a turning point; a specific point from which the escalation of natural disasters most dramatically began when compared to past periods in history.

Is there any reason or explanation for the drastic increase in tsunamis, earthquakes, floods, mudslides, destructive storms, fires, extreme temperatures, etc. since then? The figures for natural disasters have been on the upward rising ever since.

Yes, there is a reason. But only those who connect the visible facts on the ground with past histories and the reality of the infallibility of biblical prophecies in a clear-minded and unbiased fashion will the reason be apparent to.

> *And there will be signs in the sun and moon and stars; and upon the earth [there will be] distress (trouble and anguish) of nations in bewilderment and perplexity without resources, left wanting, embarrassed, in doubt, not knowing which way to turn] at the roaring (the echo) of the tossing of the sea,*
>
> *Men swooning away or expiring with fear and dread and apprehension and expectation of the things that are coming on the world; for the [very] powers of the heavens will be shaken and caused to totter.* Luke (21:25-26)

Biblical prophecies talk about a period when the world would experience catastrophic events as prophesied by the Creator Himself. These disasters that were held back so that a great purpose can be achieved will no longer be delayed once that purpose is realized. What is this purpose?

> *And this good news of the kingdom (the Gospel) will be preached throughout the whole world as a testimony to all the nations, and then will come the end.* (Matthew 24:14)

These apocalyptic events have been predestined to be held back, so a great purpose can be realized. The purpose was the global evangelization; the global spread of the Good News of His soon-coming

Kingdom on earth. After this prophecy is fulfilled, earth-shaking events will be a common phenomenon because it will no longer be delayed. It will reach a point where they will suddenly break out and shock the world with its never-before-seen scales.

The prophesied disasters were to be warning signs that the Creator God will suddenly, directly, and imminently intervene in the affairs of mankind. This is to warn those living the prevailing immoral, godless, and depraved life.

> *For nation will rise against nation, and kingdom against kingdom, and there will be famines and earthquakes in place after place.* (Matthew 24:7)

In the above passage, Jesus says that there shall be natural disasters before He returns. He went on to tell us in verse 8 that when they do start, it will only be the beginning of worst things to come—" *All this is but the beginning [the early pains] of the birth pangs [of the intolerable anguish].*" We can now see why these disasters have been rapidly accelerating and why they are likely to continue across the earth.

> *And swore in the name of (by) Him Who lives forever and ever, who created the heavens (sky) and all they contain, and the earth and all that it contains, and the sea and all that it contains. [He swore] that no more*

time should intervene and there should be no more waiting or delay. (Revelation 10:6)

The Lord told Apostle John in the above Bible passage that we would get to a period when those unfortunate events that God has been delaying will no longer be held back. We should therefore not be surprised by the increased cases of natural disasters, wars, and rumors of wars, political upheavals, economic and financial disasters, and great social and moral depravity. Jesus told us about an escalation like this, not only in number but also in intensity as we move closer to the time of His return.

With the level of technological advancement in today's world, it is safe to say the gospel has been preached in all the world or is remarkably close to it.

And this gospel of the kingdom shall be preached in all the world for a witness unto all nations; and then shall the end come. (Matthew 24:14)

We can see that all the above signs that are supposed to start when we approach the End Time have already started. What does that tell us? That means we are in the End Time.

There will be signs as we have been told and even though we will never know the exact time, we should pay attention to these things and get ourselves ready. As you watch and read the news, be alert.

But of that [exact] day and hour no one knows, not even the angels of heaven, nor the Son, but only the Father. (Matthew 24:36)

I implore you to prepare for the cataclysmic times that are ahead. Today's disasters, as unsettling as they have been, are but the beginning. There is still more to come, and it only continues. So, prepare to be a bona fide candidate of the New World that these unfavorable events will usher in.

CHAPTER EIGHT

Earthquakes

A lot of people may want to make a mockery of this one, but from all available evidence, it's crystal clear that the occurrence of earthquakes is increasing in frequency and the places of occurrence are spreading and happening in more and more places as it is stated in the Bible.

Reports released from the International Disaster Database of the Centre for Research on the Epidemiology of Disasters show a growing trend of earthquakes from 1900 to 2014. The trend is still on the upward trend even in 2019.

> *For nation will rise against nation, and kingdom against kingdom. There will be earthquakes in various places; there will be famines and calamities. This is but the beginning of the intolerable anguish and suffering [only the first of the birth pangs].* (Mark 13:8)

The Bible talks about these signs intensifying in the End Time, and that is exactly what we are witnessing with earthquakes.

Check out the following information and judge for yourself:

The report released by the United States Geological Survey (USGS) on the 23rd of April 2015 showed that 17 areas within 8 states in the U.S. have a growing trend of earthquakes, including places where they were previously not common like Northern Texas, Oklahoma, and Southern Kansas.

The Special Representative of the United Nations Secretary-General for Disaster Risk Reduction, Margaret Wahlström said in 2010, "Earthquakes are the deadliest natural hazard of the past 10 years and remain a serious threat for millions of people worldwide as eight out of the ten most populous cities in the world are on earthquake fault lines."

In 2016 alone, New Zealand experienced a record of 32,000 earthquakes.

The record shows that in just 2 years, that is, between 2014 and 2015, a millennium worth of earthquakes has taken place.

Since 2014, big earthquakes have been twofold in occurrence compared to what has been since 1979.

Between 2004 and 2014, there has been a worldwide surge in earthquakes.

Current graphs support the statistics released by USGS that shows an alarming global trend of earthquakes, increasing in both strength and frequency.

As of April 2017, the world was experiencing an average of nearly 3,500 earthquakes each month.

The devastating 7.8-magnitude earthquake of April 25, 2015 that struck a heavy blow on the capital of Nepal killed more than 7,800 people and destroyed properties.

There was a devastating earthquake in Port-au-Prince. Another destructive 7.0-magnitude earthquake took place in Contamana, Peru, in 2011.

In trying to explain away these natural disasters, most people call to science. Some say that the widespread use of earthquake detection mechanisms might have led to a global increase in trends. Some others attributed it to fracking. Fracking, which is also known as hydraulic fracturing, is a process where a pressurized liquid is used to open ground reserves for gas and oil. This practice is controversial and considered dangerous because it destabilizes the earth's structure.

Nobody is arguing against the fact that the activities of man have adversely affected the earth, but not every occurrence can be linked to this. So, everything cannot be explained with science.

One other theory suggested that the disposal of fracking wastewater deep into the ground might be responsible for these earthquakes, saying they are manmade. This theorist believes that this process is causing some pressure changes in certain areas of the earth's crust, leading to further stress on these fault lines.

The 4.2-magnitude earthquake that struck on the 2nd of May and affected Kalamazoo County, Michigan was shown to not have originated from any known fault line, and its point of occurrence was nowhere near any high-pressure injection wells that are normally used for fracking. A Western Michigan University geoscientist by the name of Chris Schmidt responded by saying the earthquake was not manmade but said that the quake is from an old fault that is under strain.

The USGS reported on April 23 that its forecasts of seismic risks for places such as Oklahoma need to be upgraded. This place has experienced 3 times as many earthquakes than California.

California is also experiencing a growing increase in daily trembler's activities. Earthquakes have been felt in San Francisco, Southern California, and Los Angeles.

The United States is not the only nation on earth with growing seismic activity. Japan's Sakurajima Island alone experienced more than 500 explosive volcanic eruptions in 2015. This figure was more than that of the previous year.

While fault lines and fracking are the reasons given for earthquakes by some people, others think its decay in morality. A Tehran prayer leader and Iranian Imam, Kazim Sadeghi on the 1st of May 2015 told his congregation that increase in earthquakes were the results of promiscuity. He then suggested taking refuge in and adapting to Islamic behavior as the only way to survive.

Although earthquakes can be linked to sin, what the Bible says is quite different from this. We are made to understand that mighty and violent earthquakes occurring in various places are signs that we are close to Christ's return.

There will be mighty and violent earthquakes, and in various places famines and pestilences (plagues: [c]malignant and contagious or infectious epidemic diseases which are deadly and devastating); and there will be sights of terror and great signs from heaven. (Luke 21:11)

There was a 6.6-magnitude earthquake that killed 193 people in China in 2015.

Two 6.0-magnitude hit Dehloran, Iran in August 2014. Another 5.4-magnitude earthquake hit in Iran in the city of Abdanan, leading to the loss of millions in damages.

Between January and May of 2015, 8 earthquakes of 7.0-magnitude took place in Alaska, Russia, the Kuril Islands, the Santa Cruz Islands, and Indonesia. Santa Cruz Islands alone had 4.

A 5.2 earthquake occurred in Ottawa, the capital of Canada. This earthquake greatly affected the Parliament building and was strong enough to spread to Toronto.

These events are God's way of warning us, and there will be no excuse if we fail to heed the warning; and if we allow the Lord's return come upon us suddenly like a thief in the night, we will have ourselves to blame and no one else.

CHAPTER NINE

Corruption: A Worldwide Scourge

The cancer of corruption has gotten to an all-time state, with complicated webs of cover-ups, deceit, and lies everywhere. We have government officials accepting bribes, corporations doctoring reports and committing account fraud, judicial system perverting justice, and education system where marks are traded for favors instead of merit—they are all signs of a society and a people on their last leg.

Widespread deceit and dishonesty twisted, and perverted languages and compromised morality are all signs of a culture whose foundation is about to give way.

We have seen presidents lie under oath, senators disgraced out of national assemblies because of corruption, organizations, and agencies that divert funds, and companies that manufacture fake and substandard products. Why is this happening, and where does it end?

Corruption has been around for nearly 6,000 years. Each government of man has had to battle this scourge. There is hardly any sphere of life that this malignancy cannot be found. It pervades every sphere of influence and can take any form, from dishonest proceedings to depravity, moral perversion, perversion of integrity, to alteration of language.

Government Corruption

One of the presidential candidates in the 2008 U.S. election vowed that he would eliminate corruption if elected. His instrument for achieving this lofty idea was with a paper clip. He planned to compare the value of any gift or benefits offered him to that of a paper clip, refuse it if the value is greater and accept it if the value is same or lower.

He didn't win, and so we did not get to know if he would have been able to keep to his words, but one thing is clear, his beautiful innovation may not be effective to fight the hydra-headed monster of corruption. Why? Officeholders have come to believe that gifts are part of the package—that is, reasonable compensation for services offered.

To think such is itself corruption. To accept gifts of significant value is a violation of public trust. When these gifts are intended to influence business decisions and influence policy, they can lead to lies. When a leader accepts bribes for his silence or support of a policy or business venture, then he can almost do anything to keep the gifts coming in.

How big is this monster?

Unfortunately, it is noticeably big, and there are way too many cases to consider. Here are a few:

The person who is perhaps America's all-time corrupt politician is Boss Tweed. He and his fellow band of thieves controlled the city of New York when the Civil War was on and after it ended. What he took home as share or commission was $200 million, which in today's exchange rate is $3.5 billion.

Siemens, a German company, had to pay $1.6 billion to the United States Justice Department for bribing Argentinian officials to win a contract in 2008.

The 2014 Winter Olympics in Sochi, Russia was said to have cost a whopping $520 million, an amount which happens to be 5 times the cost of previous Winter Olympics Games in Vancouver, Canada. The amount is nearly 350 percent over budget. It is no surprise that much of the contract was awarded to Vladimir Putin's friends and relatives.

The Beijing Olympics cost $142 million while Sochi spent $520 million. Beijing arranged 302 events while Sochi only arranged 98. You can picture the level of corruption.

Budd Dwyer, a one-time Treasurer of Pennsylvania, was asked to give out the contract for the correction of an irregularity that caused employees too much for income tax. He gave the $4.6 million contract to a California computer firm that bribed him with $300,000.

The Salerno-Reggio Calabria motorway in Italy, which was started in 1929, as of 2018, has not been completed. Over $12 billion was expended on the project in 15 years. Maintenance work in the motorway led to the death of more than 3,000 people in traffic accidents.

The Kenya Government bought pushcarts in an auction. The pushcarts were bought for the use of local farmers. This is the corruption in this case: The government said they paid $1047 for each cart, but its actual market value was $48.

The level of financial and administrative corruption in Iraq is blood-curdling. There's also heavy circumvention of the law. Government officials' resort to registering companies in the name of their friends and families when, in fact, they do not have the needed mechanisms or skilled technicians. When these fake companies finally get the chance to build hospitals, roads or schools, the results are failed projects because the amateur contractor recruits' workers and develops mechanisms or the contract is sold to another contractor; either way, it still ends in failed projects.

What Corruption Does

When corruption is tolerated and even endorsed, justice and truth are lost. Government, rather than being an institution that it is supposed to be, turns to a circus where propaganda is readily served.

Corruption causes a whole nation to be sick spiritually, right from the lowest levels of government to the highest; from those who make laws to those who enforce them. It is written in Proverbs 14:34 that, "*Uprightness and right standing with God (moral and spiritual rectitude in every area and relation) elevate a nation, but sin is a reproach to any people.*" No wonder only 3 out of 10 United States citizens trust their elected officials.

As unprecedented as corruption incidences observed in Western nations have been, they are nothing when compared to those of Asian and African countries. The whole world is soaked in the mud of this scourge.

Bribes and payoffs, in certain nations, are normal and even expected as a popular part of the culture. It is quite common in these countries for law enforcement officers to expect payment for minor infractions on the spot. Instead of nations to rent from their corrupt ways, they try to justify their actions by comparing it to those of more depraved and corrupt Third World countries.

This should not be a surprise to believers who understand the Bible. This is what God says of those who corrupt themselves, "*Ah, sinful nation, a people loaded with iniquity, offspring of evildoers, sons who deal corruptly! They have forsaken the Lord, they have despised and shown contempt and provoked the Holy One of Israel to anger, they have become utterly estranged (alienated).*" (Isaiah 1:4)

In verses 5 and 6 of Isaiah, God compares the fraudulent and crooked cultures to a wounded and diseased body, "*Why should you be stricken and punished any more [since it brings no correction]? You will revolt more and more. The whole head is sick, and the whole heart is faint (feeble, sick, and nauseated).*

From the sole of the foot even to the head there is no soundness or health in [the nation's body]—but wounds and bruises and fresh and bleeding stripes; they have not been pressed out and closed up or bound up or softened with oil. [No one has troubled to seek a remedy.]"

Mankind, all through history, in search of the perfect government has tried every conceivable form of government: monarchical, democracy, military rule, etc. We have tried all kinds of political philosophies like communism, socialism, and capitalism, but none of them have been good enough to eliminate corruption permanently. Since we left the Garden of Eden because of our disobedience, we have never found a perfect government. Even the nation of Israel, despite having God as its Head, still corrupted itself. In fact, their corruption was quick.

The world awaits a time when widely extended dishonesty will be no more, thus becoming a sound historical testimony to the pointlessness of man living according to his own rules rather than that of the Creator. Is there any hope of a time when all of mankind will deal honestly and truthfully with one another?

What Lies Ahead?

This End Time has seen the complete surrender of virtue and morality. Leaders all over the world have been breathed upon by the enticing allure of greed, lust, self-centeredness, and vanity.

Government officials trade influence for money. Businesses are founded and propagated on corrupt business dealings. The family, the basic unit of man, is gravely infiltrated with corruption, leading to the confusion of roles between father, mother, and children.

The answer to why this world of ours is filled with such disturbing levels of corruption is right in the book of Isaiah 59:2 which says, *"But your iniquities have made a separation between you and your God, and your sins have hidden His face from you, so that He will not hear."* A world separated from a fair, just, loving, and righteous God will blossom in corruption and widespread dishonesty.

Is There Any Hope?

Christ Jesus, who was here over 2,000 years ago to right the wrongs and restore our relationship with the Father, is coming back very soon to this earth. He is not coming in the form in which He came before. He is coming as a powerful King and Ruler to destroy every human government and establish a worldwide, divine government.

> *I saw in the night visions, and behold, [b]on the clouds of the heavens came One like a Son of man, and He came to the Ancient of Days and was presented before Him.*
>
> *And there was given Him [the Messiah] dominion and glory and kingdom, that all peoples, nations, and languages should serve Him. His dominion is an everlasting dominion*

which shall not pass away, and His kingdom is one which shall not be destroyed. (Daniel 7:13-14)

God will soon rid this world of corruption by eliminating the three causes of corruption: sin, satan, and status. Sin will be no more, satan will be bound and dumped in the bottomless pit, and we will have the only status we will ever need — the status of everlasting life in a new & rebuilt environment called the New Jerusalem.

Only then will the corruption end.

CHAPTER TEN

Global Crisis:
Instability Peaks

The world is coming to a close. As social unrest, together with economic turmoil, political upset, political turbulence, and turmoil reaches its peak, we draw closer to the total collapse of the world as we know it. The Lord said the earth is polluted under its inhabitants. The floods have delayed planting season which will make the harvest lessened sending the prices skyrocketing. Everything is setting in motions now.

We cannot turn on the TV without being bombarded with news about the multitude of crisis in America and different parts of the world. The overwhelming number of these increasingly regular news and stories is troubling. We hear news about Syria, Boko Haram, Iraq, ISIS, Iran, protests, evil, murder, etc.

The world's political landscape is shaking. And just as the physical tensions in the world are increasing, so also are the political and economic tensions.

ISIS continues to disturb the world with its quest for global domination and Sharia law. Their rate of killings, murder, rape, pillage, plundering, and large-scale destructive activities is not slowing down. They are propagating like wildfires all over the world. They are now in all the continents of the world.

The Syrian war has not stopped, and the terrorism and civil unrest in Africa, Indonesia, and the rest of the Middle East continues. The chaotic mess that the world has been drawn into is ever-growing with no end in sight. It is amazing the number of protests, riots, civil disobedience, or unrest that is taken place daily. Civil and political unrest and attempted overthrown of governments are all going on.

A lot of supposed houses of God are teaching heresies. Truth is being twisted or told halfway. Apostasy is now full-blown. One of the quite common signs of the End Time is apostasy. Apostasy has to do with people falling away. Just like it is prophesied in the Bible, the Church is witnessing a situation where large numbers of former devotees are abandoning, denunciating, and defecting away from their faith, and accepting a false gospel.

We now hear of Christian leaders saying that Jesus Christ is not the only way, that many other ways exist. They even tell us that God is OK with alternative lifestyles, that He does not discriminate. Now we have gay and lesbian church leaders, even Gay Bishops and Reverend Fathers. The Church has become a place of mockery. There is even what is called *Chrislam*, a union between Christianity and Islam, claiming we serve the same God. We are not surprised, as the Bible has already predicted such happenings.

> *Let no man deceive you by any means: for that day shall not come, except there come a falling away first, and that man of sin be revealed, the son of perdition.* (2 Thessalonians 2:3)

> *Now the Spirit speaketh expressly, that in the latter times some shall depart from the faith, giving heed to seducing spirits, and doctrines of devils.* (1 Timothy 4:1)

> *For the time will come when they will not endure sound doctrine; but after their own lusts shall they heap to themselves teachers, having itching ears; And they shall turn away their ears from the truth, and shall be turned unto fables.* (2 Timothy 4:3-4)

Horrible stories of fathers sleeping with their children, spouses killing one another, children poisoning their parents and young mothers throwing their babies into trash dumpsters are being aired daily.

As we preach and talk about globalization and the increase in knowledge, it is still surprising that humanity has still not changed its depraved and barbaric habits. What is the meaning of honor killings? In Pakistan alone, on the average, there are more than 1,000 deaths resulting from honor killings every year. India is also a big fan of this despicable act. How much is a life worth?

It is not that these habits were not practiced before now, but the alarming thing is their increase. Now friends and parents don't even think twice before giving up sons and daughters for these senseless killings for the simple reasons of getting married, looking at the opposite sex, wearing something the family or religion disapproves, converting to another religion, etc. It might seem unbelievable, but it is the truth. And this is mostly done for religion and culture. We are certainly in the time of Noah.

There has also been an increased rate of Christian persecution. Christians in Africa and the Middle East are being killed regularly. They are being given ultimatums to either renounce their faith or die. China continues in its practice of muzzling believers and even going as far as telling them that for serving God, they will not be allowed to enjoy certain benefits that other citizens enjoy. Hatred towards the Jews, Jerusalem and the nation of Israel is increasing.

This world is really messed up! Things are not getting better but worse. There's increased tension, violence, evil, murder, rape, hate, and crime. Radical Islamism is not receding but growing like wildfire. Natural and man-made disasters are on the increase. Epidemic and disease outbreaks have become a common occurrence. We now witness increased governmental infringement on citizens' human rights. All these signs point to one thing: a system that has failed is not working and must be replaced. It is a sign that the coming of a new and better system is not far away.

It is quite clear that the deep structural forces that are responsible for all the recent happenings have not gone away.

As the rich-poor divide grows, government dysfunction increases, and political and economic infighting rises; therefore, instability will only peak. Many more years of turmoil, socially, economically, and politically are to be expected.

And as worse and darker as things get, the world is further and further sinking into it with no hope of things getting better. This further shows that the return of Christ is closer than ever.

It was Jesus Christ who, in the Olivet Discourse, told the Apostles what the signs of His coming and that of the End Time will look like. The passage is in the book of Matthew 24:3-14, and it reads thus:

And as he sat upon the mount of Olives, the disciples came unto him privately, saying, tell us, when shall these things be? And what shall be the sign of thy coming, and of the end of the world? And Jesus answered and said unto them, take heed that no man deceives you. For many shall come in my name, saying, I am Christ; and shall deceive many.

And ye shall hear of wars and rumors of wars: see that ye be not troubled: for all these things must come to pass, but the end is not yet.

For nation shall rise against nation, and kingdom against kingdom: and there shall be famines, and pestilences, and earthquakes, in divers' places. All these are the beginning of sorrows.

Then shall they deliver you up to be afflicted and shall kill you: and ye shall be hated of all nations for my name's sake.

And then shall many be offended, and shall betray one another, and shall hate one another.

And many false prophets shall rise and shall deceive many. And because iniquity shall abound, the love of many shall wax cold. But he that shall endure unto the end, the same shall be saved.

> *And this gospel of the kingdom shall be preached in all the world for a witness unto all nations; and then shall the end come.*

Matthew 24:24 also talks about false prophets, something that is quite common today.

> *For there shall arise false Christs, and false prophets, and shall shew great signs and wonders; insomuch that, if it were possible, they shall deceive the very elect.*

Apostle Paul in 2 Timothy 3:1-5 says that the state of man in the End Time is going to get worse.

> *This know also, that in the last days perilous times shall come. For men shall be lovers of their own selves, covetous, boasters, proud, blasphemers, disobedient to parents, unthankful, unholy, Without natural affection, trucebreakers, false accusers, incontinent, fierce, despisers of those that are good, traitors, heady, highminded, lovers of pleasures more than lovers of God; having a form of godliness, but denying the power thereof: from such turn away.*

Apostle Paul also says that the doctrines of demons and deceiving spirits will cause some Christians to depart from the faith in the latter days.

> *Now the Spirit speaketh expressly, that in the latter times some shall depart from the faith, giving heed to seducing spirits, and doctrines of devils.* (1 Timothy 4:1)

We understand from the prophecy of Daniel that the End Time prophecy is being sealed until the End Time when God will open the understanding of His people; the purified, not the wicked.

> *And he said, go thy way, Daniel: for the words are closed up and sealed till the time of the end. Many shall be purified, and made white, and tried, but the wicked shall do wickedly: and none of the wicked shall understand; but the wise shall understand.* (Daniel 12:9-10).

We have experienced and are experiencing these.

CHAPTER ELEVEN

End Time Timelines

In the chapters above, we have discussed signs that show that we are in the End Time and how close we are to the return of Christ, but there are still some timelines that we are yet to experience. Some of them may have started to unfold, and others have not. Below are the End Time timelines in the correct sequence.

1. Abomination of Desolation

Knowing and understanding what the Bible says about the Abomination of Desolation is of great importance to our understanding of End Time events. Jesus told us in Matthew 24:15 and 21 that the one event that will alert God's people to the commencement of the Great Tribulation is the Abomination of Desolation.

When ye therefore shall see the abomination of desolation, spoken of by Daniel the prophet, stand in the holy place, (whoso readeth, let him understand:)

For then shall be great tribulation, such as was not since the beginning of the world to this time, no, nor ever shall be. (Matthew 24:15, 21)

2. The Great Tribulation

The Great Tribulation is well described in Matthew, chapter 24. It will be a time of great deception with false prophets and false christs parading themselves as custodians of *truth* (which is even deception).

And Jesus answered and said unto them, take heed that no man deceives you. For many shall come in my name, saying, I am Christ; and shall deceive many. And many false prophets shall rise and shall deceive many. Then if any man shall say unto you, Lo, here is Christ, or there; believe it not. For there shall arise false Christs, and false prophets, and shall shew great signs and wonders; insomuch that, if it were possible, they shall deceive the very elect. (Read Matthew 24:1-24)

It will also be a time of severe persecution and great hatred for believers. *"Then shall they deliver you up to be afflicted and shall kill you: and ye shall be hated of all nations for my name's sake. And then shall many be offended,*

and shall betray one another, and shall hate one another"
(Matthew 24:9-11).

3. The Beast and False Prophet

*And I stood upon the sand of the sea, and saw a beast
rise out of the sea, having seven heads and ten horns, and
upon his horns ten crowns, and upon his heads the name
of blasphemy. And the beast which I saw was like unto
a leopard, and his feet were as the feet of a bear, and his
mouth as the mouth of a lion: and the dragon gave him
his power, and his seat, and great authority.*
(Revelation 13:1-2)

The two principal causes of persecution during
the Great Tribulation are the Beast and False Prophet.
The Antichrist is another name for the Beast. He is
even referred to as the "little horn" in the book of
Daniel. The Beast is probably going to be a person,
but he may also be a system or organization.

4. Christ Returns to the Earth

When Christ comes, He will bring the judgment
of God (i.e., wrath) on the inhabitants of the earth as
in the time of Noah (Matthew 24:36-39). When the
floodwaters came, every soul outside of Noah's ark
died (Genesis 7:21-23). Once the door of the ark was
shut, all opportunity for salvation was forever lost to
those outside. When Christ comes, all opportunity for

the salvation of those who do not belong to Him will be lost (Revelation 9:20-21; 16:9-11).

5. The Rapture

In several passages, the Bible describes a time when Jesus will gather the people of God and remove them from the earth. This gathering is called the Rapture of the Church.

> *For the Lord himself shall descend from heaven with a shout, with the voice of the archangel, and with the trump of God: and the dead in Christ shall rise first:*
>
> *Then we which are alive and remain shall be caught up together with them in the clouds, to meet the Lord in the air: and so, shall we ever be with the Lord.* (1 Thessalonians 4:16-17)

6. The Wrath of God

A time is coming when the judgment of God will fall heavily on the world for their iniquity and for their rejection of His Son. It will be a day of great judgment and wrath.

> *And I heard a great voice out of the temple saying to the seven angels, go your ways, and pour out the vials of the wrath of God upon the earth.* (Revelation 16:1)

7. The Millennial Reign of King Jesus

Before the Great White Throne Judgment, the Lord Jesus will rule over the whole earth from the city of Jerusalem for a thousand year. He will give power to the saints to rule, together with Him, over the nations of the earth. There will no longer be wars, crying, or weeping. Wild beasts and animals will be tamed. People's life span will greatly increase, even to a thousand year.

> *And I saw an angel come down from heaven, having the key of the bottomless pit and a great chain in his hand. And he laid hold on the dragon, that old serpent, which is the devil, and satan, and bound him a thousand years, and cast him into the bottomless pit, and shut him up, and set a seal upon him, that he should deceive the nations no more, till the thousand years should be fulfilled: and after that he must be loosed a little season.* (Revelation 20:1)

8. The Final Defeat of Evil

After 1000 years satan is loosed. Immediately after the expiration of the Millennial Reign, satan is let loose from the bottomless pit for a short time so he can attempt to deceive Gog, Magog, and the nations for the final time. God weeds out any bad eggs in His Kingdom by allowing satan to tempt the people.

And when the thousand years are expired, satan shall be loosed out of his prison, And shall go out to deceive the nations which are in the four quarters of the earth, Gog and Magog, to gather them together to battle: the number of whom is as the sand of the sea. (Revelation 20:7-8)

The Final Rebellion: The devil, together with all the people he has succeeded in deceiving, will go all out, surround the city of Jerusalem, and be ready to wage war against it; but before he and his followers have the opportunity of launching an attack, he will be stopped. Fire will descend from heaven and destroy him and his invading army.

And they went up on the breadth of the earth, and compassed the camp of the saints about, and the beloved city: and fire came down from God out of heaven and devoured them. (Revelation 20:9)

After being cast into the Lake of Fire, satan is defeated: satan will then be thrown into the lake of Fire and Brimstone where he will meet up with both the false prophet and the antichrist that have previously been thrown there. The three of them will forever remain in this place, and this will be the last we ever hear from them.

And the devil that deceived them was cast into the lake of fire and brimstone, where the beast and the false prophet are, and shall be tormented day and night for ever and ever. (Revelation 20:10)

Finally, satan will get a commensurate judgment for all his deception, wickedness and evil, and for all the destruction, death, loss that he has caused. He will forever burn in the Lake of Fire.

9. The Last Judgment

The Judgment Seat of Christ according to Romans 14:10-13, which reads, *"But why dost thou judge thy brother? or why dost thou set at nought thy brother? for we shall all stand before the judgment seat of Christ. For it is written, As I live, saith the Lord, every knee shall bow to me, and every tongue shall confess to God. So, then every one of us shall give account of himself to God. Let us not therefore judge one another anymore: but judge this rather, that no man put a stumbling block or an occasion to fall in his brother's way,"* will be the examination of believers. Every work done by each believer for Christ will be laid bare and judged. Appropriate rewards will also be given to each man's work accordingly.

At the Great White Throne Judgment, all those who do not belong to God will be judged according to their deeds. All the dead, throughout history, will be brought up from the sea and Hell to be judged according to their works. The works or deeds of each person will be thoroughly examined.

After the completion of the Great White Throne Judgment, a New Heaven and a New Earth will be created.

10. Paradise Forevermore

This is the final chapter of the entire saga. After the devil has been taken out permanently, the old heaven and old earth will cease to exist, and a New Heaven and New Earth will now be in its place. The verses of the Bible below describe in exact words how our great new place with the Lord will be.

> *THEN I saw a new sky (heaven) and a new earth, for the former sky and the former earth had passed away (vanished), and there no longer existed any sea.*

> *And I saw the holy city, the new Jerusalem, descending out of heaven from God, all arrayed like a bride beautified and adorned for her husband.* (Revelation 21:1-2)

If you want to know how best to prepare for the End Time so you will not miss any of God's plans for His beloved, please read the last chapter of this book.

CHAPTER TWELVE

How Prepared Are You?

The truth is that we are a people who love to predict things. We love to predict the weather, we love to know the sex of a baby even while they are still in the womb, and we love to predict election outcomes.

Even Jesus recognized man's love for what is to come. "*He answered and said unto them, when it is evening, ye say, it will be fair weather: for the sky is red. And in the morning, it will be foul weather today: for the sky is red and lowering. O ye hypocrites, ye can discern the face of the sky; but can ye not discern the signs of the times?*" (Matthew 15:2-3)

Having foreknowledge of events that will take place over the next several years is only part of things to do to prepare for the events. From 1 Chronicles 12:32, we understand this: "*And of the children of Issachar, which were men that had understanding of the times, to know what Israel ought to do; the heads of them were two hundred;*"

and all their brethren were at their commandment." There is nothing wrong in having foreknowledge of what is to come. It feels good to know if it will rain tonight or not. We like to know if the looming thunderstorm will be heavy or light.

As good as it is to know what will take place in the future, what is more, important is the actions that we are supposed to take because of the knowledge.

Jesus Christ in Matthew 24:32 tells us the significance of signs when He says, "*From the fig tree learn this lesson: as soon as its young shoots become soft and tender and it puts out its leaves, you know of a surety that summer is near.*"

That is the essence of the signs, not to make us afraid but to teach us to respond. When we see these signs, we understand that Christ's return is near, and we prepare ourselves so we can be counted worthy.

When it comes to preparing for an incoming event, the focus of a larger percentage of people is on the aspect of physical preparation. We want to know the quantity of food we can store up, we want to know if we should move to an area where these events may not affect us, we want to know if we have saved enough money, we want to know what we can do to guarantee our safety, etc.

The problem about these types of preparation is that it is not the best preparation that we should be making, and it has questions that we cannot answer now and so cannot better prepare for. There is no way of knowing what the world's economy will look like during the Great Tribulation. It is clearly impossible to know what the availability of electricity, water, shelter, food, etc. will be like after the Sixth Trumpet War. We are more likely to have more information about what things will be like when these events begin to unfold, but not now.

All the same, spiritual preparation is our best bet and the most critical necessity, whether it is today or the next five decades. The Bible clearly gives instructions on how to prepare: *"Therefore take no thought, saying, what shall we eat? or, what shall we drink? Or, Wherewithal shall we be clothed? (For after all these things do the Gentiles seek:) for your heavenly Father knoweth that ye have need of all these things. 33 But seek ye first the kingdom of God, and his righteousness; and all these things shall be added unto you"* (Matthew 6:31-33).

Another instruction is from the book of Luke 21:36, *"Watch ye therefore, and pray always, that ye may be accounted worthy to escape all these things that shall come to pass, and to stand before the Son of man."*

Please understand that watching does not make us worthy. Our worthiness depends on our obedience to God and our relationship with Him. When we repent and surrender our life to Christ, we receive forgiveness through His blood that was shed on Calvary, and this is what makes us worthy to stand before God without sin or guilt.

Amid knowing what is coming, and spiritually preparing for it by surrendering our lives to Christ, there is still more to do. Jesus tells us in Matthew 15:3 to *discern the signs of the times* and watch for what is happening. This will not only give us inner peace and trust in God's ability to see us through, but it will also provide us with the needed sense of urgency.

If we faithfully and carefully watch for the signs, we will know when the *fig tree is blooming*, or when God's Kingdom is at hand.

To once again emphasize it, the best thing anybody can do to better prepare him or herself for future events like Rapture, the Second Coming of Christ, the New Heaven and a New Earth, etc., is to be born again. "*Jesus answered and said unto him, Verily, verily, I say unto thee, except a man be born again, he cannot see the kingdom of God*" (John3:3).

Maybe you are thinking within yourself, "But I have done some awful things, and I can say that I'm beyond saving or redemption."

That is not so. Here is the answer to your concern.

The name "Jacob" literally means a "deceiver" or "crook." This name accurately describes the character of Jacob. In Genesis 27:19-24, he purposefully lied and deceived his father Isaac, not once but three times, and stole the blessings meant for his twin brother Esau. This wicked deception drove him into a twenty-year exile. When he discovered, on his way back home, that his brother was coming with 400 men, being filled with fear, guilt, terror, and shame, he called unto God. He ran to God, knowing his brother was going to kill him.

On that fateful night, he wrestled with the Angel of God. He refused to let go until something was done to change his condition. And according to his prayers, his situation was reversed. God gave him a new name. He received a new nature, a new name, a new heart, and a new character because he was humble enough to know his sins, serious enough to repent of them, and had enough faith to cry to God and believe He could change his situation.

Another story of Jesus changing the life of someone who was already condemned is that of

Zacchaeus (Luke 19:1-10). He was a fraudulent tax collector. He was overtaxing and stealing from people. He took from people by falsely accusing them. He was not a good person. Tired of his deceit, lies, stealing, and bad reputation, he went in search of the person who alone could change his situation. He went in search of Jesus.

On the day of his salvation, he climbed unto a Sycamore tree so he could see Jesus. Fortunately for him, it was Jesus who looked up and saw him. This shows that if we will only humble ourselves and run to Jesus, He is ever ready to forgive and cleanse us. The tax collector confessed his many sins, repented of them, and went ahead to make restitution. He gave half of his wealth to the poor; and to anybody he had once cheated, he restored fourfold.

The very same experience that changed Jacob to Israel and Zacchaeus the tax collector to an honorable man is the same that can change your life for the best, no matter the level of decay it has gone through. This discovery is of very significance, even more than the discovery of electricity. This discovery can help us in ways electric light cannot.

We all are by nature, sinful, deceptive, crooked, wicked, coldhearted, etc. You may have discovered while going through this book, that your life has been like these people. You know you have lied, committed murder, stolen, and falsely accused others. The thought of all the bad things that you have deliberately done is terrifying to imagine. And the Bible says in Romans 6:23, *"for the wages of sin is death; but the gift of God is eternal life through Jesus Christ our Lord."* Every worker of iniquity will find themselves outside of the New Jerusalem according to Revelation 22:15, *"For without are dogs, and sorcerers, and whoremongers, and murderers, and idolaters, and whosoever loveth and maketh a lie,"* and they shall be thrown into the lake of fire and brimstone according to Revelation 21:8, *"But the fearful, and unbelieving, and the abominable, and murderers, and whoremongers, and sorcerers, and idolaters, and all liars, shall have their part in the lake which burneth with fire and brimstone: which is the second death."*

Despite our depraved nature, Christ still loves us. On the cross of Calvary, He gave His life for all our sins. He rose from the dead after three days and ascended to Heaven. He is now at the right hand of the Father pleading with us to forsake our life of darkness and embrace that of light before it is too late. Soon, this world will be utterly consumed by fire (Revelation 18:8). This world will soon witness an unthinkable degree of devastation it has never seen before.

Today is your night of wrestling with an angel. Today is when the Master will come into your home— your heart. We are now at the breaking of the day according to prophecy. The time of the coming of the Son of God is almost upon us. Our prayer now should be that God will break us the same way His messenger touched the hip of Jacob and come into our house just like He visited Zacchaeus. May He pulverize every inch of wickedness that lies deep within us. And if we can, in simple faith, call upon Him and ask for His mercy, He will, through His boundless love and grace, save our soul.

We have seen that End Time biblical prophecies are being fulfilled in our lifetime, showing more and more that we are living in the last days of human history. Prophecies given thousands of years ago are coming into manifestation in our time and generation. This means that we are on the eve of the last days and we do not have much time left to second guess or make jest of this. This world of great evil and sin is about to end in a fiery and loud conflagration, with a spectacular New World put in its place by the Lord Jesus Himself. It only takes a simple act of faith for you to become a member of this new Kingdom.

In John 14:14, Jesus says, *"I am the Way and the Truth and the Life; no one comes to the Father except by (through) Me."* Now is your accepted time of salvation.

Now is the time to escape everlasting damnation and enjoy paradise forever

A Clarion Call

To receive salvation, I implore you to pray this prayer of faith with me:

Dear God,

I come to You in the Name of Jesus. Your Word says, "Whosoever shall call on the name of the Lord shall be saved" (Acts 2:21). I call on You now and ask You to forgive me of all my sins. The Bible says if I confess with my mouth that "Jesus is Lord," and believe in my heart that God raised Him from the dead, I will be saved (Rom. 10:9). I believe with my heart and I confess with my mouth that Jesus is the Lord and Savior of my life. You also said in Your Word, "If ye then being evil, know how to give good gifts unto your children: how much more shall your heavenly Father give the Holy Spirit to them that ask him?" (Luke 11:13). I am also asking You to fill me with the Holy Spirit. Holy Spirit rise within me as I praise God. Thank You for saving me!

In Jesus' Name, I pray. Amen.

Have you just prayed the salvation prayer with your whole heart?

I congratulate you for coming into the Family of the LORD.

About the Author

Lee Edward Gaddie is a native of Little Rock Arkansas. After a stint in the U.S. Army, he gave his life to the Lord and began serving Him. Then, in 1979, he answered the call to full-time ministry. For some years, he pastored Whole Truth Temple Church of God in Christ in several locations in Hensley and North Little Rock, Arkansas, but his ministry eventually took him to the Houston, Texas, where he founded and still pastors The New Jerusalem Whole Truth Church located in Humble, Texas. He also oversees several other churches.

Apostle Gaddie was ordained a bishop under the leadership of Bishop James McNeal, Jr., the founder of the New Hope and Faith Church based in Philadelphia. Apostle Gaddie and his wife, Prophetess Pearly (Ragland) Gaddie, are the parents of seven children and the grandparents of sixteen. (Pictured above: Apostle Gaddie and his wife.)

To Our Readers

Our **readers** are our most important resource. We value your suggestions, testimonies, and fellowship! If you are ever in the Houston (Texas) area, please feel free to join Apostle Gaddie the N.J.W.T.C. Family by visiting:

The New Jerusalem Whole Truth Church

6524 Bender Rd. | Humble, TX 77396

(281) 533 – 3651

Sundays 11am – 1pm & 8pm – 10pm

Wednesdays 7:30pm – 9:30pm

Fridays 8pm – 10pm

Additional Book Resources

Apostle Gaddie and his wife, Prophetess Pearly Gaddie, are the authors and/or contributors of several published books.

If you would like to order additional copies of this book or a copy of one of their other titles, please call (281) 533-3651 to order a copy. You may also write or visit:

The New Jerusalem Whole Truth Church

6524 Bender Rd. | Humble, TX 77396

(281) 533 – 3651

---

*The Commander's Anointing

by Apostle Lee E. Gaddie

From There to Here: A Prophetic Journey of Faith and Obedience

by Prophetess Pearly Gaddie

Book descriptions on following pages

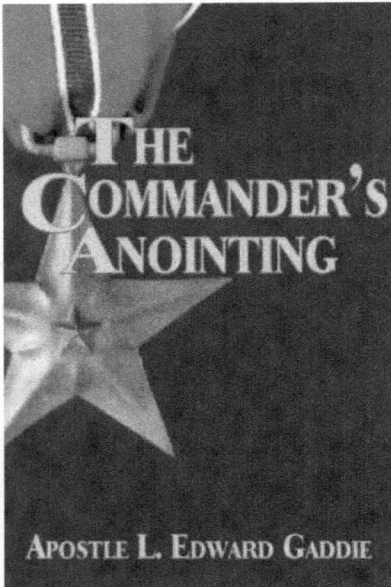

The Commander's Anointing

Joshua spoke to the sun, and it stood still in the sky and stayed there until the battle he was waging could be won. How did he do that? Elisha spoke to a borrowed axe head that had sunk beneath the water of a stream, and it floated to the surface and was retrieved. How did he do that? Samson caught three hundred foxes, tied their tails together, lit them, and sent them scurrying into the standing cornfields of the enemy Philistines. How did he do that? Jesus spoke to the winds and waves, and they obeyed Him. How did He do that?

In this powerful and anointed book, Apostle L. Edward Gaddie answers these and other important questions, showing how God, the great Commander of all Commanders, has chosen certain men and women to bear a special anointing, an anointing to do the impossible. This is…The Commander's Anointing.

From There

To Here

Just as God called Abraham to leave his home and his people and go to a land he knew not of, God called the Gaddie family in Arkansas. Strangely enough, it would be ten years before they even knew where they were to go. Once that became known, they immediately began their journey of faith. But this would not be an easy journey. Along the way, there would be severe tests of their faith, and they would have to believe God to show them each next step and to provide for their large family as they took those steps. There were moments when it seemed like they would surely perish and others when it seemed that they could not endure the hardness of the tests. But with every step and every trial overcome, they learned something new and wonderful about the God who had called them on this journey of faith and obedience. Here, in the pages of this book, Prophetess Pearly Gaddie tells, for the very first time, how they got "From There to Here" and how God kept them during their journey.